PENGUIN

A Mid

CLAUDIA RODEN was born and brought up in Egypt. The publication of her *Book of Middle Eastern Food* in 1968 revolutionized Western attitudes to the cuisines of the Middle East. She continued to write cookery books with a special interest in the social and cultural background of the food. Her books have won her many awards. The Glenfiddich Trophy was given 'In celebration of a unique contribution to the food that we eat in Britain today'; the Prince Claus Award for Culture of the Netherlands was in recognition of exceptional achievements. In 2010 the James Beard Foundation of America inducted Roden into the Cookbook Hall of Fame for the influence her first book has had on cooking in America.

A Middle Eastern Feast

CLAUDIA RODEN

PENGUIN BOOKS

PENGUIN BOOKS

Published by the Penguin Group
Penguin Books Ltd, 80 Strand, London WC2R 0RL, England
Penguin Group (USA) Inc., 375 Hudson Street, New York, New York 10014, USA
Penguin Group (Canada), 90 Eglinton Avenue East, Suite 700, Toronto, Ontario,
Canada M4P 2Y3 (a division of Pearson Penguin Canada Inc.)
Penguin Ireland, 25 St Stephen's Green, Dublin 2, Ireland
(a division of Penguin Books Ltd)
Penguin Group (Australia), 250 Camberwell Road,
Camberwell, Victoria 3124, Australia
(a division of Pearson Australia Group Pty Ltd)
Penguin Books India Pvt Ltd, 11 Community Centre,
Panchsheel Park, New Delhi – 110 017, India
Penguin Group (NZ), 67 Apollo Drive, Rosedale, Auckland 0632, New Zealand
(a division of Pearson New Zealand Ltd)
Penguin Books (South Africa) (Pty) Ltd, 24 Sturdee Avenue,
Rosebank, Johannesburg 2196, South Africa

Penguin Books Ltd, Registered Offices: 80 Strand, London WC2R 0RL, England

www.penguin.com

A Book of Middle Eastern Food first published 1968
Revised edition, *A New Book of Middle Eastern Food*, first published 1985
This extract, with a new introduction, published in Penguin Books 2011

1

Copyright © Claudia Roden 1968, 1985, 2011
All rights reserved

Set in 10.75/13 pt Berkeley Oldstyle Book
Typeset by Jouve (UK), Milton Keynes
Printed in Great Britain by Clays Ltd, St Ives plc

Cover design based on a pattern from a seventeenth-century Iranian dish. Fritware
with polychrome underglaze painting. (Photograph copyright © Victoria & Albert
Museum.) Picture research by Samantha Johnson. Lettering by Stephen Raw

ISBN: 978–0–241–95111–8

www.greenpenguin.co.uk

MIX
Paper from
responsible sources
FSC™ C018179

Penguin Books is committed to a sustainable
future for our business, our readers and our
planet. This book is made from paper certified
by the Forest Stewardship Council.

Contents

Introduction (2011)

I started collecting recipes for *A Book of Middle Eastern Food* when Jews left Egypt after the Suez crisis in 1956. I was at art school in London, and my parents followed my brothers and me there. During the next decade I saw waves of relatives and friends who stopped over in the city. Everyone was asking for recipes and offering theirs. We might never see each other again, but we would have something to remember each other by. The women who gave me recipes were, like my mother, in their late forties and older. They said that they had them from their mothers and grandmothers. So the ways of cooking had not changed for at least a hundred years. I took down everything they said: 'you know that there is enough flour when the dough feels like your earlobe'; 'rub the toasted hazelnuts with your hands then go out in the garden and blow the skins off'; 'mince the meat three times through a fine mincer then pound it to a paste'. Every recipe was precious. There had been no cookbooks in Egypt, and we were all concerned with keeping a link with the life we left behind.

Egypt in our time had been a very mixed cosmopolitan society in the cities (it was the time of King Farouk and I saw in Gamal Abd el Nasser's revolution). There were long-established communities of Armenians, Greeks, Italians, Syrians and Lebanese, as well as expatriate

French and British communities. Our royal family was an Ottoman Albanian dynasty and our aristocracy was Turkish. The Jews were also mixed. My grandparents came from Syria and Turkey, and there were families from North Africa, Greece, Iraq and Iran. When we ate at friends' homes we enjoyed a range of dishes from various countries. That is why I ended up covering most of the Middle East.

We were very Europeanized. We spoke French at home and Italian with our nanny. At the English School in Cairo we studied English history and geography, nothing at all about Egypt or the Arab world. But generations of my family had lived for hundreds of years an integrated life in the Arab and Ottoman worlds, and something of their sensibilities, experience and knowledge filtered down to us. It was those worlds that captivated me – the part of my culture that I hardly knew, which belonged to my parents, especially my father – that I wanted to recapture. That is why I filled the book with Arab proverbs, riddles, tales and poems about food. I am sometimes asked how a Jewish woman can be fascinated with Arab food and culture. I reply that they were also ours and we were part of it.

At the British Library I found a translation of a thirteenth-century culinary manual from Baghdad, accompanied by poems celebrating food translated by Professor Arberry, and a social analysis by the French orientalist Maxime Rodinson of a culinary manuscript of the same period from Damascus. Some medieval recipes had similar names, similar combinations of ingredients and flavourings, and similar techniques to those I had been hearing from the people who were giving me their recipes. I was enthralled. For months I entertained friends with medieval banquets. That is how I became interested in the history of food.

After the publication of the book, people always talked to me about food. Those who came from the Middle East revealed their passions for particular foods and offered culinary secrets. I was invited to eat and to watch people cook and I had correspondents in different countries. My pockets were full of cooking instructions acquired at chance meetings, and my drawers were full of recipes written in different hands. I also had many opportunities to travel in the Middle East. I went on collecting recipes and researching the background of the dishes. The new material went into a 1985 edition entitled *A New Book of Middle Eastern Food*. The extracts in this little book are from that edition.

Although I made some changes and additions throughout the 1985 edition, I left the recipes as they were with the voices and idiosyncrasies of those who gave them. The amateur way in which they are described reflects the rich and varied character of very personal and much-loved cooking traditions passed down through generations in the family. It was cooking without gadgetry. Even when I was trying out the recipes there were no food processors or blenders. In the second edition, after explaining a laborious method, I sometimes added that you could do it all very quickly and easily with a food processor. That is what I suggest you do when you need to blend something to a paste.

The history, tales poems and proverbs are not

included in this book. The editors chose to feature only the narrative extracts that are in my voice. That voice is the one I had as a young woman whose mother tongue was French, beginning a new life in a new world and missing the old one, writing to record a lost heritage in a country where people asked if Middle Eastern food was about sheep's eyes and testicles.

Introduction (1968)

[. . .]

The first recipe I wrote down was for *ful medames*. I was a schoolgirl in Paris then. Every Sunday I was invited together with my brothers and a cousin to eat *ful medames* with some relatives. This meal became a ritual. Considered in Egypt to be a poor man's dish, in Paris the little brown beans became invested with all the glories and warmth of Cairo, our home town, and the embodiment of all that for which we were homesick.

Our hosts lived in a one-room flat, and were both working, so it was only possible for them to prepare the dish with tinned *ful*. Ceremoniously, we sprinkled the beans with olive oil, squeezed a little lemon over them, seasoned them with salt and pepper, and placed a hot hard-boiled egg in their midst. Delicious ecstasy! Silently, we ate the beans, whole and firm at first; then we squashed them with our forks and combined their floury texture and slightly dull, earthy taste with the acid tang of lemon, mellowed by the olive oil; finally, we crumbled the egg, matching its earthiness with that of the beans, its pale warm yellow with their dull brown.

[. . .]

It has been, for me, a matter of great delight to acquire an extra recipe from some relative passing through London, a well-known ex-restaurateur from Alexandria, or somebody's aunt in Buenos Aires – another treasure to pass on to the Middle Eastern community in Paris, Geneva or Milan.

Friday night dinners at my parents, and gatherings of friends at my own home, have been opportunities to rejoice in our food and to summon the ghosts of the past.

Each dish has filled our house in turn with the smells of the *Muski*, the Cairo market, of the *corniche* in Alexandria, of Groppi's and the famous Hati Restaurant. Each dish has brought back memories of great and small occasions, of festivals, of the emotions of those times, and of the saying invariably said. They have conjured up memories of street vendors, bakeries and pastry shops, and of the brilliant colours and sounds of the markets. Pickles and cheeses have re-created for us the atmosphere of the grocery shop round the corner, down to which a constant flow of baskets would be lowered from the windows above, descending with coins, and going up again with food. It is these smells, emotions, habits and traditions, attached to and inseparable from our dishes, a small part of our distinctive culture, that I have tried to convey with the food.

At first, on leaving Egypt, I imagined our food to be uniquely Egyptian. In Europe, I discovered that the Turks claimed most of our dishes, and that the Syrians, Lebanese and Persians claimed the rest, leaving us with only a few specialities, our 'national dishes'. Nearly all our food was common to other Middle Eastern countries, so to write about 'our food' was to write about Middle Eastern food generally. I have not been able to disentangle what is an Egyptian culinary tradition from a Turkish, Persian or Syrian one, and I have had to include various countries which I did not intend to at first, but which were necessary to make a complete and comprehensible picture of what was originally my 'family's food'.

[. . .]

Middle Eastern food was in fashion a long time ago. Interest in the cuisine has mirrored the relationship between Europe and the followers of Islam and the relative prestige of their two cultures. It has depended on war and peace, on politics and commerce and also on the spirit of Europe, whether it cultivated the senses or denied them, whether it was hedonist or puritan. In the full-blooded Middle Ages when Islam was in its Golden Age with the most advanced civilization in the world, Middle Eastern food had the greatest impact on cooking in Europe.

At that time Christian Europe looked on the Infidels with fear and horror as pillaging and ravaging barbarians and cruel despots, but at the same time it was impressed by their wealth and power. Chroniclers wrote of the magnificent courts and of the loves and excesses of the Caliphs. Travellers and merchants told of the extraordinary and exquisite foods they were served while they sat on a rug near a fountain in a fruit garden. While worrying about the odious enemy, Europe fantasized about its fabulous riches, of harems and serails, bazaars and minarets, about fierce warriors who chopped off heads, and passionate lovers. The Crusades created an even more avid interest, a mixture of hate for the enemy and fascination for its exotic culture. Popular curiosity was captivated by the philosophical and scientific knowledge of the Islamic civilization. The courts and the upper classes imitated its ways and its fashions. The cooking, too, was a stimulus and an inspiration which brought new ways of looking at food.

When commerce flourished between East and West, rice, almonds, pine kernels and other nuts and dried fruits, such as prunes, raisins, apricots and dates, arrived from the Levant with the aromatics which play an important part in Oriental cooking. Rose water and orange blossom essence, tamarind and all types of seeds, plants and bark appeared in Europe. The Crusaders, Orientalized by years spent in the Levant, often with a local cook in their employ, brought home the ways of handling them. There are still traces of this early influence in the most English of foods: in Christmas pudding and mince pies, marzipan, and in rice pudding, and it is a curious thought that our famous brown sauces and the mint and vinegar sauce for lamb perpetuate the lustre of ancient Persia on our everyday tables.

In the last few years I have become increasingly aware of the debt owed by early European cookery to the Arab tradition. I have come across recipes here and there in old English and French cookery books which are almost identical to those featured in early Islamic manuscripts. They make use of rice and ground almonds or milk of almonds, of the same mixtures of spices and aromatics and the whole range of dried fruits and nuts which were part of the early trade with the Levant [. . .].

Flavourings, Condiments and Perfumes

No one who has walked through a Middle Eastern spice street can ever forget the intoxicating effect of mingled scents nor the extraordinary displays of knotted roots, bits of bark and wood, shrivelled pods, seeds, berries, translucent resins, curious-looking plants, bulbs, buds, petals, stigmas, even beetles.

Practically every main town in the Middle East has its *attarine* or spice street in the *soukh* or bazaar, where rows of very small shops (some as small as cupboards) sell spices and aromatics. Vendors lay them out with art to tempt those passing by with their delicate shades of gold and brown and their enigmatic shapes. They sometimes roast, grate or crush them to a powder in a mortar, on demand, and sift them through a fine sieve as they did centuries ago. They fill little cones made out of tightly rolled pieces of newspaper and offer them as though they were magic potions.

The Orient is renowned for its delight in incense, perfumes and aromatic flavourings. Since early times it was part of the spice route between the Far East, Central Africa and Europe. The local taste for spices and for sweet dishes was inherited from Ancient Egypt and the Graeco-Roman world when spices are thought to have been used also to mask the smell of slightly 'off' meat. Long before Islam, Arabia was already known as the land

1

of spices, and Herodotus wrote that the whole country was scented with spices and exhaled a marvellously sweet odour. The country, however, was only the transit area – as were Persia and Ethiopia – for the transport trade between East and West when spices were the most highly prized merchandise because of their small volume and high prices. Their commerce which was kept going in a small way even throughout the Muslim conquests flourished especially during the Crusades. The middlemen, Arabs, Persians and Saracen merchants (the last mainly Syrians and Jews), fiercely guarded their monopoly and their sources of supply. Saracen ships brought spices from China, Tibet, Malacca, Java and Sumatra as well as India and Ceylon and the east coast of Africa through the Persian Gulf and the Red Sea. Trading posts were established everywhere and when the Arab conquests interrupted business relations with Europe, the Jews became the middlemen. Goods were transferred to camels following the caravan routes through the Arabian desert to Palestine and Syria, or came via Cairo in boats on the Nile. Trading ships waited in the Mediterranean to carry them into Europe through the ports of Venice and Genoa. It is not surprising that the intermediaries should have succumbed to the attractions of their precious merchandise. A certain magic still surrounds the use of spices and aromatics, which are not only used for their taste but also for their medicinal, therapeutic and even sometimes aphrodisiac value. For they are variously believed to increase the appetite, help digestion or calm the nerves, to be good for the heart and circulation, to be antitoxic or sexually stimulating and even to kill microbes. Attributes are well-founded or romantic; ginger is said to make people loving, rose water to give a rosy outlook, dill and aniseed to have digestive qualities, and garlic to be both health-giving and an antiseptic.

Almost everything that can add a touch of flavour or aroma is used in cooking. The aromatic plants most commonly used are flat-leafed parsley, coriander (sometimes called 'Arab parsley') and mint. Oregano, wild marjoram, thyme and dill, fenugreek, bay, celery, fennel, chives and tarragon, purslane and rue also play their part. Herbs are so popular that they are sometimes placed in a bunch on the table for people to pick at. Fresh coriander is used liberally in salads as well as stews, mint marries happily with yoghourt, dill is especially popular in Turkey and Iran.

All the usual spices come into use: saffron, turmeric, cumin, coriander, cinnamon, nutmeg, allspice, cloves, ginger, cardamom, caraway, aniseed, sesame, poppy seed, fennel, dill, fenugreek and mustard seeds, peppercorns, cayenne and paprika – all these have an important place. Each country has its favourites and its own special mixtures and combinations. In Egypt it is garlic fried with cumin and coriander; in Turkey it is cinnamon combined with allspice. Syrians and Lebanese love sumac and the sweet-and-sour flavour of tamarind and also pomegranate molasses. North Africans use much preserved lemon and both sweet and hot ground red peppers, while Moroccans have a range of savoury dishes that include saffron, ginger, cinnamon, and cumin as well as hot red pepper and honey.

3

SOME LESS COMMON FLAVOURINGS

BOIS DE PANAMA (also called saponaria) is a pale dry wood which, when boiled in water, produces a thick white foam. It is used to make the cream called *naatiffe* for *karabij*.

MAHLAB is black cherry kernels and gives a special taste to breads and pastries. It is sometimes sold already ground.

MASTIC (sometimes wrongly called gum arabic, which is glue). The hard resin of the lentisk tree that grows on the greek island of Chios is sometimes used as chewing gum with a little piece of ordinary wax to soften it. It must be pulverized by pounding it with a pinch of sugar before it is used to flavour puddings.

MUSK, which comes from the abdominal scent glands of the male musk deer of the Himalayas, gives a heavy scent to puddings. Abel – musk seeds (*ambrette*) are a substitute flavouring.

ORANGE BLOSSOM WATER lends a delicate perfume to syrups, pastries and puddings. You may add a drop or two to water and Turkish coffee, a tablespoonful to a salad dressing or a stew. A teaspoon in a coffee cup of boiling water, with or without sugar, makes the soothing and digestive 'white coffee' of Lebanon. Only a diluted form of the strong distilled essence is obtainable in this country. It was used here a good deal as a flavouring centuries ago but in recent years has been sold as a toiletry article by chemists.

PEPPERS. Many types of peppers are used. Besides the black pepper berry and the weaker white pepper seed freed from its powerful wrinkled black skin, there are grey peppers called cubebs and long peppers which look like a black catkin, both of which are not as strong as the black berries. All these are best bought whole and used freshly ground. There is also the dried red pepper or pimento of which there are many varieties – all of the capsicum family. Dried and ground it ranges from the mild, sweet red pepper and paprika to the very fiery cayenne or chilli powders.

POMEGRANATE SEEDS. The juicy, shiny pink seeds of the fresh fruit are sprinkled on salads and on tahina sauce for fish. Cut the fruit in half, scoop out the seeds and discard the bitter-tasting pith. Dried wild seeds give a sharp flavour to hummus and tahina.

POMEGRANATE MOLASSES (also called SYRUP) are made from the juice of sour rather than sweet fruits boiled down to a thick syrup.

ROSE BUDS. A powerfully aromatic variety of rose from Damascus is used to perfume strong spice mixtures. In Egypt we used to leave rose buds about in little plates to embalm the air.

ROSE WATER, produced by boiling rose petals and condensing the steam, is used to scent syrups, pastries and puddings and all types of hot and cold drinks. Often used together with orange blossom water, when it is the weaker of the partnership and can therefore be used less sparingly.

SAHLAB – the bulb of a type of orchid – is used in powder form to thicken milk and lend it a special flavour.

SHAMAR in Arabic, *mavro* in Greek, is found here in Indian shops as onion seed. It is mixed in among sesame seeds on bread and *kahk*.

SUMAC (or *summak*) is a sourish, dark, browny-red spice made from the coarsely ground dried berries of the sumac shrub. Iranians use it frequently and provide it in restaurants particularly to flavour kebabs. Iraqis use it too and Lebanese and Syrians sprinkle it on salads or on fish. Juice can be extracted by soaking cracked seeds (about 120 g/4 oz) in 350 ml (12 fl oz) of water for 20 minutes, then straining and squeezing the juice out. It is often used instead of lemon juice.

TAMARIND. You can find this in Indian shops, sold partly dried as a sticky mass of broken pods with fibres and seeds. Macerated in hot water these produce a sour, dark brown juice. Used with sugar it gives a pleasant sweet and sour taste.

A commercial paste and tamarind balls are easier to use and a reasonably good substitute.

TAHINA PASTE is the oily meal which results from crushing sesame seeds. It is used both raw and cooked for sauces.

LEMONS PRESERVED IN SALT. The French name for this North African speciality is *citrons confits*. It is much used as a condiment to flavour chicken dishes and all sorts of stews and sometimes to enliven a salad. Use ripe lemons or limes. Wash them well. Cut them in four – in two if they are limes – but not right through. Let them hold together at the stem end. Sprinkle salt inside the slits. (Use about 120 g (4 oz) salt for 1 kg (2 lb) lemons.) Put them in a wide-necked jar. Press the lemons down hard with a weight like a stone (well washed). The salted juices which are gradually released, augmented by the juice of other lemons, preserve the peels which soften and mellow and are ready in a month. You may use them whole or chopped up or the peel alone without the pulp. The juice can be used as a seasoning.

NOUMI BASRA (IN IRAQ) OR OMAN LEMONS (IN IRAN). These small, brown, dried limes which give a sharp musty flavour to Iranian and Iraqi soups and stews can now be bought whole or ground in some Indian and Oriental stores, but you can make them yourself by letting fresh limes dry out. It takes several months for them to be completely dry and hard and very dark brown inside. The time depends on the weather. It is best to put them out in the sun to begin with and leaving them on radiators also helps. They are ready when they sound hollow when you tap them on the table. You may use them whole – pierced with a fork when the skin softens with cooking, or cracked open with a hammer or a pestle and mortar, in which case people who are specially fond of them may like to have them in their serving. Otherwise you may add them in ground form. One lime is usually enough for a stew for 6.

DIBBIS, or date syrup, is an Iraqi sweetening agent made by boiling dates until they form a pulpy mass. In the past it was poured into a basket strainer. Another basket was inverted over this and they were placed between two boards by means of which the juice was expressed. (People stood and jumped on top.) It was then poured on to trays, allowed to evaporate in the sun and the thick syrup which resulted was stored in tins and jars.

The syrup, which looks like thick brown treacle, keeps well and is used in savoury as well as sweet dishes. It is not easy to find here at the moment. People like to mix it with tahina and eat this with bread.

SAMNA (clarified butter) is also used for its distinctive flavour. To clarify butter, heat it slowly in a pan until it is thoroughly melted and bubbling, then chill it until it is firm. Transfer carefully to another pan leaving behind the residue at the bottom. Melt the butter again and when it froths strain it through a fine cloth into a jar.

Make a large quantity, it keeps for months (actually, years). It gives a special acid taste to food and does not burn.

Some people flavour the butter as it bubbles with aromatics such as fenugreek, caraway or cardamom seeds. Use 1–2 tablespoons of seeds to 250 g (8 oz) butter.

SPICE MIXTURES

Every household has favourite spice mixtures which they blend to taste and keep in jars as a ready condiment or flavouring. A few are made to be eaten with bread. This is broken into pieces, dipped in olive oil and then in the condiment to pick it up.

There are classic mixtures which vendors make up and which are often simply called 'the three spices' or 'the four spices'. In Egypt what we called *les quatre épices* was a ground mixture of cloves, cinnamon, nutmeg and pepper. 'Four spices' in Tunisia may mean cinnamon, pepper, rose buds and paprika, and in Morocco it may be cloves, nutmeg, ginger and pepper. 'Curry mixtures' of varying compositions popular in the regions neighbouring India are similar to those of that country.

RAS EL HANOUT. Grocers in North Africa stake their reputation on a 'house blend' which according to folklore may contain up to a hundred aromatics but in reality contains around twelve. The 'grocer's head', as it is called, generally includes cinnamon bark, whole nutmeg, dried rose buds, pieces of dried ginger, cloves, cubebs and different peppers – sometimes the golden green Spanish fly, renowned for its 'aphrodisiac' qualities. They are pounded together in a mortar as required.

ZAHTAR. A mixture of thyme and salt or *sumac*, which occasionally contains toasted sesame, is sold in little paper cornets to dip bread into.

RELISHES

Some spice mixtures are made into a paste with oil or tomato concentrate or something moist. A covering layer of oil stops them spoiling.

HARISSA. This hot chili pepper paste flavoured with garlic and spices is much used in North African cooking. It can be bought ready-made in tubes and cans but it will not have the special perfume of the home-made variety. To make your own: soak 50g (2 oz) dried hot red chili peppers (stems and seeds removed) in water for 30 minutes until soft. Drain and pound in a mortar or blend in the food processor with 4 garlic cloves, 1 teaspoon ground caraway, 1 teaspoon ground coriander, ½ teaspoon salt, adding just enough extra virgin olive oil, by the tablespoon, to make a soft paste. Press into a jar and cover with oil.

TABIL. A Tunisian mixture of fresh coriander, caraway seeds, garlic and red peppers, both sweet and fiery, ground or pounded to a paste.

ZHUG. I tasted this relish in Israel, where it was brought by Yemenite immigrants. It is so strong that a tiny drop picked up on the tip of my little finger set my throat on fire.

Grind and blend the following to a paste: 1 teaspoon black pepper, 1 teaspoon caraway seed, 3–4 cardamom pods, 4 strong dried peppers soaked in water for an hour, 1 whole head garlic, a good bunch of coriander leaves and salt. Use it to flavour soups and stews or simply to dip your bread in.

Mezze

Mezze are one of the most delightful features of Middle Eastern food – not least because they are meant to be enjoyed in an unhurried way – indeed they are almost a way of life. From the cafés by the Nile to mountain resorts in the Lebanon and palatial villas in Morocco and Persia, savouring *mezze* with an ouzo, a beer, a syrup or a coffee can be a delight approaching ecstasy, part sensual, part mystical. The pleasure of savouring the little pieces of food is accompanied by feelings of peace and serenity, and sometimes by deep meditation.

HUMMUS BI TAHINA
Chick Peas with Tahina

This tahina salad is the most widely known and appreciated of all outside the Middle East. It makes an excellent appetizer served as a dip with bread, fish, aubergines – practically anything – and can also be used as a salad with a main dish.

250 g (8 oz) chick peas, soaked overnight
Juice of 2–3 lemons, or to taste
2–3 cloves garlic, crushed
Salt
150 g (5 oz) tahina paste

GARNISH
1 *tablespoon olive oil*
1 *teaspoon paprika*
1 *tablespoon finely chopped flat-leaf parsley*

Boil the soaked chick peas in fresh water for about 1 hour, or until they are soft. The cooking time will depend on their age and quality. Drain them, reserving the cooking water, and put aside a few whole ones to garnish the dish. Blend to a puree in a food processor or blender, adding the lemon juice and a little of the cooking water. Add the remaining ingredients and blend to a creamy paste, adding more water if necessary. Keep tasting and adjusting the seasoning, adding more lemon juice, garlic or salt if necessary.

This is one of the dishes which, for centuries, have been traditionally decorated in the same manner. Pour the cream into a flat serving dish and dribble a little red paprika mixed with olive oil over the surface. Sprinkle with chopped parsley and arrange a decorative pattern of whole chick peas on top.

Serve as a dip with Arab bread or pitta.

≈ An alternative, rather hotter cream is made by using a generous pinch of cayenne pepper instead of paprika. Some of it is mixed into the cream, the rest is sprinkled over the top together with a little ground cumin, in a star design of alternating red and brown.

≈ Pine nuts, toasted, or sautéed in a little butter, make a very special garnish, or you can sprinkle with ground *sumac* and a little chopped parsley.

BABA GHANOUSH
(ALSO CALLED MOUTABAL)
Aubergines with Tahina

This rich cream is a combination of two strong flavours: the smoky one of aubergines prepared as below, and the strong taste of tahina sharpened by lemon and garlic. It is exciting and vulgarly seductive. The ingredients are added almost entirely to taste, the harmony of flavours depending largely on the size and flavour of the aubergines used.

The quantities below give a fairly large amount, enough to be served as a dip at a party.

3 large aubergines
2–4 cloves garlic, crushed, or to taste
Salt
180 ml (¼ pint) tahina paste or less, depending on the size of
  the aubergines
Juice of 3 lemons, or more to taste
½ teaspoon ground cumin (optional)
2 tablespoons finely chopped flat-leaf parsley
A few black olives or 1 tomato, thinly sliced,
  to garnish

Cook the aubergines over charcoal or under a grill, turning them until they feel soft and the skin blackens and blisters (or roast them in a hot oven until they feel soft). Peel and wash them, and squeeze out as much of the juice as possible.

Blend the aubergines to a rough purée in a food processor. Add the crushed garlic and a little salt.

Add the tahina paste and lemon juice alternately, blending for a few seconds between each addition. Taste and add more salt, lemon juice, garlic or tahina if you think it necessary, and if you like, a little cumin.

Pour the cream into a bowl or a few smaller flat serving dishes. Garnish with finely chopped parsley and black olives, or with a few tomato slices. Serve as an appetizer with Arab or other bread, as a salad, or as a party dip.

BOILED CARROT SALAD

This is a fiery Moroccan salad. Make it with old carrots, which taste better. Add the flavourings gradually, to taste. The colour is beautiful. Serve as a dip with bread or bits of raw vegetables.

> 500 g (1 lb) carrots
> Salt and pepper
> ½–1 teaspoon harissa, or 1 teaspoon paprika and a good pinch
>   of cayenne
> 1–2 teaspoons cumin
> 3 tablespoons wine vinegar
> 4 tablespoons extra virgin olive oil
> 2 cloves garlic, crushed
> ¼–½ teaspoon ground ginger
> A few olives to garnish

Peel the carrots and boil in salted water until very soft. Drain and mash with a fork in a bowl and stir in the rest of the ingredients or, better still, turn to a smooth purée in a blender.

Serve cold garnished with a few green or black olives.

≈ Alternative additional flavourings are 2 tablespoons honey and 1 teaspoon cinnamon.

DUKKAH

This is a dearly loved and old Egyptian speciality. It is a loose mixture of nuts and spices in a dry, crushed but not powdered form, usually eaten with bread dipped in olive oil. In Egypt it is served at breakfast time, as an appetizer, or as a snack in the evening. It is a very personal and individual mixture which varies from one family to another. Here is my mother's.

500 g (1 lb) sesame seeds
250 g (8 oz) coriander seeds
120 g (4 oz) hazelnuts
120 g (4 oz) ground cumin
Salt and pepper to taste – try 1 teaspoon salt and ½ teaspoon
    black pepper

Roast or grill the ingredients separately. Pound them together until they are finely crushed but not pulverized. The crushing can be done in a mincer or an electric blender. In the last case run it for a very short time only, as otherwise the oil from the too finely ground seeds and nuts will form a paste with the pulverized ingredients. *Dukkah* should always be a crushed dry mixture, and definitely not a paste.

The quantities above make a good deal of *dukkah*, but it can be stored for many weeks in covered jars.

≈ Another very humble preparation, a mixture of dried crushed mint, salt and pepper, is sold in the streets in little paper cornets as *dukkah* to sprinkle over bread.

Savoury Pastries

In his *Kanju'l Ishtiha* (Treasure of the Appetite) the fifteenth-century Persian poet of food, Abu Ishaq of Shiraz, wrote: 'We came into the kitchen for this purpose, that we might show the fried meat to the pastry.'

The Middle East has 'shown to the pastry' not only meat, but also chicken, brains, cheese, eggs, spinach, aubergines and all the nuts they have had available.

Savoury pastries are one of the most interesting features of Oriental food. *Sambusak, börek, pasteles, bstilla, fila, brik, spanakopitta, lahma bi ajeen* are a vast family of glorious little pastries, half-moon shapes, triangles, fingers, small pots, little parcels of all types, as well as medium-sized pies and enormous ones. Various doughs are used, each country and community favouring a particular type; and to make it more confusing, different names are given to the same pastries by different countries and communities, while sometimes the same name can apply to two very different pastries.

SANBUSAK

At a banquet given by the Caliph Mustakfi of Baghdad in the tenth century, a member of the company recited a poem by Ishāq ibn Ibrāhīm of Mosul describing *sanbūsaj* (*sanbusak*) as 'This tastiest food for hurried diner-out'.

Here is a modern recipe for *sanbusak*, popular in Syria, the Lebanon and Egypt. The recipe for the dough has for centuries been explained as 'one coffee cup of oil, one coffee cup of melted butter, one coffee cup of warm water, one teaspoon of salt. Add and work in as much flour as it takes.' Translated into English weights and measures, it is:

DOUGH
120 ml (4 fl oz) oil
120 g (4 oz) butter, melted
120 ml (4 fl oz) warm water
1 teaspoon salt
500 g (1 lb) plain flour, sifted
1 egg, beaten
Sesame seeds (optional)
Clarified butter for shallow-frying or oil for deep-frying

CHEESE FILLING
500 g (1 lb) crumbled feta cheese
2 lightly beaten eggs
3–4 tablespoons chopped mint leaves

To make the dough: put the oil and butter together in a small heatproof bowl, and heat over boiling water until the butter has melted. Mix with warm water and salt, and pour into a large mixing bowl.

Add flour gradually, stirring slowly with a knife and then your hand, until the dough forms a soft, rather greasy ball. A few tablespoons more flour may be required. The dough should be handled as little as possible, so stop mixing as soon as it holds together.

Traditionally, *sanbusak* are half-moon-shaped. Either roll the dough out thinly on a floured board and cut into rounds about 8 cm (3 inches) in diameter with a pastry -cutter, or take walnut-sized lumps and flatten them out as thinly as possible between the palms of your hands.

Put a heaped teaspoonful of filling in the centre of one half of each circle. Fold the other half over to make a half-moon shape and seal by pinching the edges tightly. If you like, make the traditional festoon-type edge by pinching and folding over all along. Arrange on baking sheets, which need not be greased.

Brush the surface with beaten egg and, if you like, sprinkle lightly with sesame seeds. Bake in a preheated slow to moderate oven (160°–180°C/350°–375°F/Mark 3–4) until they are a pale golden colour, about 35 to 45 minutes. Alternatively, fry gently in clarified butter until golden and well cooked inside, which takes only a few minutes, or deep-fry in oil. In this case, do not brush with the egg and water mixture.

Serve hot or cold, but preferably just out of the oven, when they are at their best. Depending on the size of the *sanbusak*, this quantity makes about 30 pastries.

≈ Here is a similar alternative dough: work the oil and creamed butter into the flour, and add milk instead of water gradually until the dough becomes a ball and leaves the sides of the bowl. In this case, too, do not work the dough longer than necessary.

MOROCCAN CIGARS

These are called *briouats* in Morocco, where they are made with paper-thin pancakes called *ouarka*, but *filo* makes an easy and perfect substitute. They are elegant party fare that you can make by the hundred (perhaps with the help of your children) and keep uncooked in the freezer. In Morocco they are fried but it is much easier and just as good to bake them.

The most popular filling is meat. For 500 g (1 lb) filo, prepare the following minced meat filling:

> 1 medium onion, finely chopped
> 4 tablespoons oil
> 750 g (1½ lb) lean minced beef or lamb
> 2 teaspoons cinnamon
> ½ teaspoon allspice
> ¼ teaspoon ground ginger
> Salt and pepper
> Pinch of cayenne or, more optionally, a bunch of flat-leaf
>   parsley, finely chopped, or a bunch of fresh coriander,
>   finely chopped (or both)
> 5 eggs
> 180 g (6 oz) butter, melted

Soften the onion in the oil. Add the meat and crush it with a fork. Add seasonings and spices and cook, stirring with a wooden spoon, for 10 to 15 minutes until the meat is done. Add the herbs. Lightly beat the eggs in a bowl and pour them over the meat. Cook gently, stirring all the time, for a minute or so until the eggs have set to a creamy consistency. Let the filling cool. Add more spices and pepper if you like.

To roll the cigars: cut each sheet of *filo* into three rectangles and put them together in a pile so that they do not dry out.

Brush very lightly with melted butter.

Put a tablespoon of filling along one of the short edges, roll the *filo* over it, tuck the ends in to stop the filling falling out, then continue to roll up like a cigar. Place side by side on a greased tray, brush with melted butter and bake in a preheated slow oven (150°C/300°F/ Mark 2) for ½ hour or until golden. Serve very hot.

≈ In Morocco they like dusting them with caster sugar or with cinnamon.

≈ If you want to fry a few for an instant snack (they are nice fried) do so in hot oil, turning over once, until browned, and drain on absorbent paper.

LAHMA BI AJEEN

A brilliant dish – an Arab type of pizza with a meat filling. Delicious, dainty, elegant to serve at a party, these savouries are very easy to prepare with a simple bread dough.

A few years ago, my brother met a well-known ex-restaurateur from Alexandria in a cinema queue in Paris. He brought back from this encounter detailed instructions on how to make *lahma bi ajeen* – to our unanimous delight. My mother has made them on numerous occasions since, usually in large quantities. She uses a dough

made with 1 kg (2 lb) flour to serve 20 people easily.
I am giving smaller quantities to serve about 8 to 10.

DOUGH
15 g (½ oz) fresh yeast or 7 g (¼ oz) dried yeast
Scant 300 ml (½ pint) lukewarm water
Pinch of sugar
500 g (1 lb) plain flour
1 teaspoon salt
2 tablespoons oil

Dissolve the yeast with a pinch of sugar in about 150 ml
(¼ pint) of the lukewarm water specified above. Leave
aside in a warm place for about 10 minutes, or until the
mixture begins to bubble.

In the meantime, sift the flour and salt into a large
warmed mixing bowl. Make a well in the centre and add
the oil and the yeast mixture. Work the dough vigorously, adding the remaining lukewarm water gradually,
enough to make a soft dough. Knead vigorously for
about 15 minutes until the dough is pliable and elastic,
and comes away from the sides of the bowl. Cover with
a damp cloth and set aside in a warm, draught-free place
for 2 to 3 hours, or until doubled in bulk. To prevent a
dry crust forming on the surface, put a very little oil in
the bottom of the bowl and roll the ball of dough in it to
coat the entire surface before leaving it to rest.

While waiting for the dough to rise, prepare the
filling:

500 g (1 lb) onions, finely chopped
Oil

750 g (1½ lb) lean lamb or beef, minced
500 g (1 lb) fresh tomatoes, skinned and chopped, or a 400-g
   (14-oz) tin skinned tomatoes
1 small tin tomato concentrate
1 teaspoon sugar
¾ teaspoon ground allspice
1–2 tablespoons lemon juice
Salt and black pepper
3 tablespoons finely chopped parsley (optional)
Pinch of cayenne pepper (optional)

Soften the onions in a little warm oil until they are transparent and have lost their water, taking care not to let them colour. Mix the meat, tomatoes and tomato concentrate in a large bowl. If you are using fresh tomatoes, get rid of as much of their juice and seeds as possible, and crush them to a pulp. If you are using a tin of tomatoes, drain them well, as too much liquid will make the dough soggy. Add sugar, allspice and lemon juice, and season to taste with salt and pepper. Drain the onions of oil and add them to the meat mixture. Knead well by hand. Some people like to add chopped parsley and a little cayenne pepper as well.

The filling is sometimes varied by omitting the tomatoes altogether, and adding 60 g (2 oz) pine nuts and 2 to 3 tablespoons tamarind juice or 2 teaspoons tamarind paste.

Knead the risen dough a few times and divide it into many walnut-sized balls. Allow to rest for a few minutes, then roll each piece on a lightly floured board with a lightly floured rolling pin into a round flat shape 12 to

15 cm (5 to 6 inches) in diameter. Alternatively, oil your hands lightly, take smaller lumps of dough, and flatten each piece as much as possible with the palm of your hand on an oiled plate.

Spread the prepared filling very generously over each piece, covering the entire surface (otherwise the filling will look meagre when the pastries are baked). Transfer each round to a lightly oiled baking sheet as you prepare it. Let them rest for 10 minutes.

Bake in a preheated very hot oven (230°–240°C/450°–475°F/Mark 8–9) for 8 to 10 minutes only. The pastries should be well done but still white and soft enough to roll up or fold in the hand to be eaten, as some people like to do.

≈ For people in a hurry an improvised *lahma bi ajeen* can be made with an opened-out pitta bread instead of the dough.

≈ Delicious pies called *s'fiha* have yoghourt mixed with the meat instead of tomatoes.

BSTILLA

Pronounced 'pastilla', this is one of the Moroccan dishes said to have been brought back by the 'Moriscos' from Andalusia after the *Reconquista*.

'Food for the Gods', as it is described by Moroccans, this magnificent pigeon pie is baked on special occasions, such as when entertaining important guests. Its gentle harmony is achieved by contrasts – it is juicy and crisp, sweet and salty at the same time.

This is my favourite version from Fez of a small *bstilla* made with chicken, and without eggs. I use filo pastry instead of *brik* (paper thin pancakes). The sheets I use measure about 48cm × 30cm. If you can only find narrower sheets, such as the ones measuring 30cm × 18cm now available in supermarkets, you can have them overlapping. Wrap any sheets that are left over in clingfilm and keep in the refrigerator for future use. Serves 4 to 6.

> 2 large onions, sliced (about 500 g/1lb)
> 3 tablespoons olive or sunflower oil
> 50 g (2 oz) blanched almonds
> ½ teaspoon ground ginger
> 1½ teaspoons cinnamon
> 300 g (10 oz) skinless chicken thigh fillets
> Salt and black pepper
> Large bunch coriander, chopped (about 75g/3 oz)
> 7 large sheets of filo (about 200 g/7 oz)
> About 75 g (3 oz) butter, melted
> 1 egg yolk
> To decorate: icing sugar and cinnamon

Put the onion in a wide saucepan with 2½ tablespoons oil and cook, with the lid on and stirring occasionally, over a low heat, for about 30 minutes until it is very soft; the onion will steam in its juice.

In the meantime, fry the almonds in the remaining drop of oil, stirring and turning them over, until slightly browned, then drain on kitchen paper and chop them coarsely.

When the onion is beginning to colour, stir in the ginger and cinnamon, then put in the chicken cut in bite-size pieces, and season with salt and pepper. Cook, uncovered, stirring occasionally, for about 15–20 minutes, until the onions are pale gold. If by this time there is still some liquid left (which would make the pastry soggy), remove the chicken pieces and continue to cook the onion until the liquid has evaporated and you can see the oil sizzling. Now return the chicken, add the coriander and mix very well.

Open out the sheets of filo when you are ready to use them and leave them in a pile so they don't dry out. Brush the top one with butter melted in a small pan.

Fit the first sheet in a greased round baking pan about 24 cm (9½ inches) in diameter and brush it entirely with melted butter, pressing the filo into the corners with the brush and letting the longer edges hang over the sides. Repeat with 4 sheets, brushing each with melted butter first, including the ends that overhang the sides at different points (again, to prevent them from drying out).

Spread the chicken and onion mixture evenly in the hollow, then bring the overlapping filo up over the filling to cover it. Sprinkle all over with the chopped almonds.

Lay another sheet of filo over the top, brush it with melted butter, then lay the final sheet. Do not brush the last sheet with melted butter. Cut the longer overhanging ends of the sheets in a curve, leaving a wide margin round the pan. Now tuck these edges into the sides of the pan around the pie. Brush the top with egg yolk mixed with a drop of water. Bake the pie in an oven preheated to 180°C/350°F/Mark 4, for 30–40 minutes until it is puffed up, crisp and golden. Now put the pie on the bottom surface of the oven for about 15 minutes, which will help to brown the bottom.

Serve the pie hot, dusting the top with icing sugar and then making a geometric pattern in the white icing sugar with the golden-brown cinnamon.

≈ For a version from Tetouan, add the juice of ½ lemon and the chopped peel of ½ preserved lemon (see page 6) to the filling. In this case, do not sprinkle the top of the pie with sugar or cinnamon.

Soups

In the Middle East, soups are often eaten as a meal in themselves, accompanied by Arab bread or pitta, for breakfast, lunch or supper. Vendors sell them in the street in the very early hours on winter mornings to catch those who want to fill themselves up before they get to work. Rich with vegetables, meat, pulses, cereals and rice, they are sometimes indistinguishable from stews, except for the fact that they have very much more liquid. They are often cooked for so long that you can no longer distinguish what is in the pot. Some of the richer soups play a part in the rituals of religious festivals, and are called 'festive' or 'wedding' soups. A few are Ramadan specials.

Calf's feet or sheep's feet are added for their gelatinous quality. Pulses – lentils, chick peas, yellow split peas, dried green peas and haricot and broad beans – lend themselves beautifully to make thick, creamy soups, delicately enhanced by spices, lemon, garlic and fresh herbs. There are infinite combinations of spinach and lentils, spinach and meat balls, yoghourt and barley, yoghourt and spinach, and so on. Chicken stocks are sometimes thickened with beaten egg yolks and lemon, and fish stocks with egg yolks and vinegar, while meat stocks are made richer with a marrow bone.

Some of these soups and stews were branded as 'servants' food' by the rich, Europeanized Egyptians, who preferred cosmopolitan food. Most of these families gave their servants a daily sum with which to buy themselves, say, 2 piastres' worth of meat and 1 piastre's worth of vegetables. These were put in a large pot and left to cook over a very low flame on a primus stove or *fatayel* on the roof-tops of the luxury blocks of flats, where the servants' quarters were usually situated. Sometimes all the servants of one block pooled their purchases or money to make one large, communal dish. The strong aromas enveloped the street below, drowning the limper, delicate perfumes of their masters' refined dishes.

The rich defended themselves from the accusation that they ate well while their servants had only cheap food, by saying that the latter *preferred* their own food. There was a great deal of truth in this, and I know many children of rich families who would sneak up to the roof terraces to share their servants' soups and stews.

MELOKHIA

Melokhia is one of Egypt's national dishes. It is an ancient peasant soup, the making of which is believed to be portrayed in Pharaonic tomb paintings. The medieval *melokhia* seems to have been a little richer, incorporating fried minced meat and chicken balls. Today, only a few families add these.

This soup has all the qualities of the Egyptian peasant: his timelessness, his harmony with nature, the seasons and the soil. It seemed to us as children that the *fellah* was the same as he was when he first appeared in history. He wears the same clothes, uses the same tools, and daily repeats the same movements as did the peasants depicted in the Pharaonic tomb paintings and described in Coptic legends. In his present lies the past. The *fellah* gives himself entirely to the soil; in return, the soil yields to him his food. Every peasant, however poor, has a little patch of ground for his own use, and in summer this is reserved exclusively for the cultivation of the deep green *melokhia* leaf (*corchorus olitorius*). The leaves can be eaten fresh, or dried and stored for the winter.

Peasant women prepare this soup almost daily. Protein stock is too expensive, so they cook the leaves in water in which a few vegetables have been boiled. The leaves give the soup a viscous texture. The women cook the soup in large pots, which they carry to the fields on their heads for the men to eat at midday. When the work is done and the men come home, they eat it again at dusk with equal pleasure.

Melokhia has recently acquired a symbolic and patriotic importance in Egypt, for it represents the national, popular taste as opposed to the more snobbish and cosmopolitan taste of the old régime. Most families have their own special way of preparing it, and the proportions vary according to the financial means, position and preferences of the people who make it.

2–2½ litres (3–4 pints) *chicken, rabbit, goose, duck or meat*
    stock (see method)
Salt and black pepper
1 kg (2 lb) frozen melokhia, defrosted
2–3 cloves garlic

Salt
2 tablespoons butter or oil
1 tablespoon ground coriander
Cayenne pepper

To make the stock: boil a whole chicken or rabbit, half a goose, a duck, or a piece of lamb, beef or veal (I suggest knuckle of beef or veal) for 2 to 3 hours, removing scum from time to time. Season with salt and pepper.

Remove the bird or piece of meat, bone it if necessary, and discard the bones.

Strain the stock into a large saucepan and bring to the boil. Add the *melokhia* and stir well. Boil for 5 to 10 minutes.

Prepare the *taklia* (garlic sauce). Crush the garlic with a little salt, using more or less garlic as you prefer. Fry it in butter or oil (in Egypt *samna*, a clarified butter, is used) with the coriander and a good pinch of cayenne pepper, stirring until the aroma rises.

Add this to the soup, cover the pan tightly, and simmer for a further 2 minutes. Stir occasionally to prevent the leaves from falling to the bottom, and do not overcook for the same reason. The *melokhia* should stay suspended throughout the stock. Taste and adjust the seasoning.

This can be served on its own first, as a soup, then accompanied by plain rice (which can be cooked in some of the stock), and finally with pieces of the meat used for making the stock, cut into serving pieces and reheated.

≈ An embellishment if you like is to start off with a richer stock by adding 2 leeks, 2 turnips, 2 tomatoes, skinned and quartered, 1 onion and a clove of garlic at the beginning. When the stock has cooked for a few hours, remove the vegetables together with the meat, and proceed as described above.

LENTIL SOUP

There are several versions of this favourite winter soup made with red lentils.

It can be made with water, but a meat or chicken stock will make it considerably richer and tastier.

3 tablespoons oil
1 large onion, chopped
1 stalk celery with leaves, chopped
1 carrot, chopped (optional)
375 g (12 oz) red lentils, washed if necessary
2 litres (3½ pints) chicken or meat stock or water
1 marrow bone (optional)
Salt and black pepper
Juice of ½–1 lemon (optional)
1 teaspoon ground cumin (optional)
Small garlic-flavoured croûtons (see method) (optional)

Soften the onion, celery and carrot, if used, in oil in a large saucepan. Add the lentils, water or stock and the marrow bone which, if cracked, will release even more marrow; bring to the boil and skim if necessary. Simmer gently, covered, until the lentils disintegrate.

Season the soup with salt and pepper and, if you like, add a little lemon juice and cumin. Simmer for a few minutes longer, then remove the marrow bone. Add a little water if you want a lighter soup, or evaporate by simmering a little longer to reduce and thicken it.

Serve with small croûtons of bread fried in oil to which a clove or two of crushed garlic has been added just as they begin to turn golden brown. Garlic is not always used, but I feel that, fried and aromatic, it enhances the taste of the lentil cream.

≈ A good variation for a rather liquid soup is to add about 60 g (2 oz) washed rice and simmer for about 20 minutes, or until the rice is just tender. Or 60 g (2 oz) vermicelli may be added in the same way.

≈ An alternative flavouring to the cumin and lemon juice is to stir in, just before serving, a *taklia* sauce, made with 2 or 3 crushed cloves of garlic, fried with 1 tablespoon ground coriander seeds.

HARIRA
Moroccan Soup

During the thirty days of the fast of Ramadan, every household prepares its own version of this national soup. The smell permeates the streets of Morocco long before sunset, when it is time to break the fast. You may add some meat cut into cubes, and some bones, to this meatless version.

This makes enough for 15 to 20 people.

250 g (8 oz) chick peas
250 g (8 oz) haricot beans or other beans

33

250 g (8 oz) large brown or green lentils, rinsed
1 large tin peeled tomatoes
500 g (1 lb) onions, coarsely chopped
Salt and pepper to taste
1 tablespoon turmeric, or to taste
Juice of 1 large lemon, or more
3–4 tablespoons flour
1 small bunch fresh coriander, finely chopped
1 small bunch flat-leaf parsley, finely chopped
120 g (4 oz) cooked rice (optional)
1 teaspoon harissa (optional)

Wash and soak the chick peas and beans for a few hours or overnight. Drain. Bring them to the boil in fresh cold water in a large pan and simmer until tender. Add the lentils and continue to cook until these are just tender. Add the tomatoes, cutting them up into small pieces, the onions and more water. Season to taste with salt and pepper, add turmeric (some people use saffron instead) and lemon juice and simmer a further ½ hour.

In a small pan stir 600 ml (1 pint) cold water gradually into the flour, beating constantly so as not to have any lumps. Add some strained liquid from the hot soup and stir over low heat until it begins to boil. The flour gives the soup a velvety texture much loved in Morocco. Add the chopped coriander and parsley leaves and pour back into the soup.

Continue to cook until the pulses are soft and the taste is rich. Adjust the seasoning and add water if necessary. Add the rice just before serving and *harissa* if you like.

Fish

In some parts of the Middle East fish is still believed to have magical properties. Tunisians in particular believe it to be highly beneficial. The day after their wedding, couples are encouraged to step over a large fish as an assurance of happiness and a protection from evil. Today, the shape of a fish has become a symbol. Embroidered on material and carved in metal, it is believed to ward off the evil eye. In Egypt, one felt compelled to eat fish for the first meal in a new home. In Persia, fish is eaten on New Year's Eve to cleanse the people from evil, while Jews display the head alone in the centre of the New Year table in the hope that Jews will always be at the 'head'.

The medieval cookery manual of al-Baghdadi gives a few recipes for fish, both fresh and salted, but without specifying any varieties. Even today, recipes for fish can often be applied to any of a number of varieties. When asking which fish should be used for *cousbareia, sayya-diah* or *blehat samak*, I was inevitably told 'any fish you like' or 'any fish will do'. Nevertheless, certain fish are more suitable for a particular dish, if only because of their size and oiliness. Their distinctive flavours and affinities also make them natural favourites for certain methods of preparation; but it is always possible to sub-stitute a similar one if a particular kind is unobtainable.

These recipes were, of course, most often evolved for fish from the Mediterranean and neighbouring seas. Most popular are the red mullet, called *barbunya* by the Turks and *Sultan Ibrahim* by the Arabs; the grey mullet; a fish called *morgan* or *arous*, which is the French *daurade*, and whose closest English equivalent is the sea bream; the sea bass, called *loukoz*; and the sole, called *samak Moussa* after Moses (because of its thinness it is said to have been cut in half when Moses separated the Red Sea). Turbot, cod, sardines, tuna, John Dory, gurnard and swordfish abound in the seas of the region.

Of the freshwater fish, a type of trout called *chaboute* is fished in the Tigris and Euphrates rivers. It is usually smoked by a fire to make *masgouf*, a popular Iraqi speciality. Carp is a Turkish fresh-water favourite, and shad is a popular fish found in the rivers of North Africa. Fish from the Nile are considered hardly fit to eat as they are impregnated with the strong taste and smell of the Nile mud.

Ever since ancient times, salted and dried fish has been known in all parts of the Middle East. This was originally done to preserve the fish so that it could be stored and taken on long journeys, or sent to regions far away from the coast. Today, it is prepared in this way primarily because people like it so much. Methods vary in detail but are basically the same. The fish is washed and cleaned and split open. It is salted inside and out and left to dry in the hot sun, or else it is buried in the hot sand or mud for a few days to 'mature'. The result is called *fessih*.

CHERMOULA
A Moroccan Marinade for Fish

Every town, even every family, has a special combination for this marinade in which every type of fish, big or small, whole, filleted or cut in chunks, is left to absorb the flavours. Different herbs are used – parsley instead of coriander, spices in varying proportions, onion instead of garlic – so you may feel free to use the following list of ingredients as a guide and suit your taste.

It is marvellous and I strongly recommend it, but not for a fish with a delicate flavour.

The following measures make a rather large quantity but it keeps well for several days if covered by a thin layer of oil.

> *1 large bunch fresh coriander, very finely chopped*
> *1 large bunch flat-leaf parsley, very finely chopped*
> *6 large cloves garlic, crushed*
> *1 tablespoon cumin*
> *1 teaspoon coriander*
> *1 tablespoon paprika*
> *1 very good pinch cayenne*
> *Juice of 1 or 2 lemons, or 150 ml (¼ pint) vinegar*
> *300 ml (½ pint) olive or other oil*

Beat all the ingredients well together. Scale, gut and clean the fish if necessary and marinate for at least an hour (you may leave it overnight). If the fish is large, put some of the marinade inside as well.

≈ For grilled fish brush the marinade on as the fish is on the grill. Serve with lemon wedges.

≈ For fried fish roll the marinated fish in flour, fry in clarified butter or in deep hot oil until browned. Serve with lemon wedges.

≈ For a baked fish put it in the oven in an earthenware dish, pour the marinade over it and bake slowly, covered with a lid or foil (they like it a little overcooked in Morocco).

≈ You may serve *chermoula* as a sauce.

TARATOR BI TAHINA
Tahina Sauce for Fish

The most popular Arab sauce for fish is made with tahina. You can serve it with fried and grilled fish as well as with a cold fish.

300 ml (½ pint) tahina
150 ml (¼ pint) lemon juice, or more
50–90 ml (2–3 fl oz) water
Salt
2 cloves garlic, crushed

Beat the lemon juice and then the water into the tahina. It will stiffen at first and then become smooth. Add only enough water for a light cream. Season to taste with salt and beat in the garlic.

Serve in a separate bowl.

SAMAK TARATOR
Fish with Tarator Sauce

This is a great gala dish, particularly popular in Egypt, Syria and the Lebanon. It is usually served lavishly decorated in a variety of brilliant colours and traditional designs according to local taste. Today it is sometimes replaced on special occasions by the French *poisson à la mayonnaise*, or decorated in a more European manner.

Choose a large fish such as sea bass, bream or John Dory. Have it scaled and cleaned. Leave the head on. Rub all over with salt, pepper and olive oil, and bake in an oiled baking dish or wrapped in foil.

Serve the fish cold on a large dish on a bed of parsley or lettuce. Decorate it with lemon slices, sliced green pickles, black olives, radishes, fried pine nuts or almonds, and pieces of pimento. Make an Oriental design, for example a criss-cross pattern.

Accompany with bowls of *tarator* sauce made as follows:

2 slices white bread, crusts removed
250 g (8 oz) pine nuts (ground almonds will do if these are unobtainable or too expensive)
1–2 cloves garlic, crushed with salt
Juice of 1–2 lemons, or more
Fish stock left over in baking dish or foil, or water

Soak the bread in water and squeeze it dry. Blend the pine nuts in a food processor. Add the bread and blend them together. Add crushed garlic, lemon juice and enough fish stock or water to blend to a smooth creamy paste.

≈ A delightful version of this dish is boned fish *tarator*. Prepare the fish and bake it in foil. Allow to cool. Cut off the head and tail neatly and set aside.

Skin and fillet the fish. Season to taste with salt and pepper. Place the re-shaped fish on a large serving dish, patting it back into its original shape. Place the head and tail at each end and mask the whole body of the fish with *tarator* sauce.

Serve decorated with whole pine nuts or almonds, lightly fried, pickles, olives, and whatever else you like.

This method of boning and reassembling the fish is particularly useful if dealing with a very large fish that does not fit into the oven. It can be cut into manageable pieces instead, and then baked in foil as usual.

Poultry

In the villages of most Middle Eastern countries, where it requires an *eid el kibir* or very important feast to kill a lamb, poultry is the usual festive dish. Geese, ducks, hens or fat chickens are the festival queens.

Often they are boiled first to provide the legendary wedding or other festive soups, and in Egypt, the *melokhia* (see page 29). They are served beautifully decorated and flavoured in an extraordinary variety of ways. Sometimes they are filled with rich stuffings before they are boiled.

Every day, the trams and buses coming into the towns from the villages are crowded with peasants carrying crates of live, cackling poultry. The chickens are killed and plucked at the market or poultry shops. In Egypt, it is common practice for peasants and shopkeepers to push a large handful of corn down the birds' throats before killing them so that they weigh more.

COLD CHICKEN SOFRITO

A dish of the Jews of Egypt, prepared on Friday to be eaten cold on Saturday.

1 large chicken
2 tablespoons sunflower oil

Juice of ½–1 lemon
½ teaspoon turmeric
Salt and white pepper
1 cardamom pod, cracked

Wash the chicken and wipe it dry.

In a large saucepan or flameproof casserole put the oil, lemon juice, a coffee cup of water, turmeric, salt and white pepper, and the cardamom pod. Bring to the boil, then place the chicken in the pan. Cover and cook over very low heat, turning the chicken over frequently and adding another coffee cup of water as the liquid is reduced. Continue cooking until the chicken is very tender. Adjust the seasoning. Remove the pan from the heat and allow to cool.

Divide the chicken into joints, removing the larger bones and the skin and arrange in a deep serving dish. Pour the sauce over it and allow it to become quite cold. On cooling, it will become a pale, lemony jelly and the chicken will be a very delicate off-white. If you prefer an absolutely clear jelly, simply skim any fat off the surface before pouring it over the chicken. Use absorbent paper to remove the last traces.

This is a very simple and delicate way of cooking chicken. Serve as part of a cold buffet, or for a family meal in summer, accompanied by salads.

CHICKEN WITH OLIVES

Preserved lemons add a special touch to this Moroccan *tagine*. If you find the olives too salty, soak them in 2 changes of water for one hour.

3 tablespoons olive oil
2 onions, grated or very finely chopped
½ chilli pepper, finely chopped (optional)
2–3 garlic cloves, finely chopped
A pinch of saffron threads or saffron powder
½–¾ teaspoon ground ginger
1 chicken, jointed
Salt and pepper
Juice of ¼-½ a lemon
2 tablespoons chopped coriander
2 tablespoons chopped parsley
peel of 1 large or 2 small preserved lemons, cut into strips
12–16 green or violet olives

In a wide casserole or heavy-bottomed pan that can hold the chicken pieces in one layer, heat the oil and put in the onions and the chilli. Sauté, stirring over low heat, until the onions are soft, then stir in the garlic, saffron and ginger.

Put in the chicken pieces, season with salt and pepper, and pour in about 300 ml (½ pint) water. Simmer, covered, turning the pieces a few times and adding a little water to keep them covered. Lift out the breasts after about 20 minutes and put them aside. Continue to cook the remaining pieces for another 20 minutes then return the breasts to the pan.

Add the lemon juice, the chopped coriander and parsley, the preserved lemon peel and the olives and simmer uncovered for 10 minutes, until the chicken is very tender and the sauce is thick and unctuous.

PERSIAN CHICKEN STUFFED
WITH DRIED FRUITS

1 large chicken
1 onion, finely chopped
Butter
250 g (8 oz) prunes, soaked, stoned and chopped
250 g (8 oz) dried apricots, soaked and chopped
60 g (2 oz) seedless raisins
2 apples, peeled, cored and chopped
Salt and black pepper
1 teaspoon ground cinnamon

Fry the chopped onion in 2 tablespoons butter until soft and golden. Add the chopped fruits and raisins and sauté gently for a few minutes. Season to taste with salt, pepper and cinnamon.

Stuff the chicken with this mixture. Rub it with salt and pepper and place it breast-down in a baking tin. Wrap extra stuffing in a piece of foil and put it in the oven with the bird. Roast in a preheated oven (190°C/375°F/Mark 5), allowing about 25 minutes per 500 g (1 lb). Baste frequently with melted butter and turn over after 1 hour.

HAMAM MESHWI
Grilled Baby Pigeons (Squab)

One of the happiest and most popular outings of my childhood in Cairo was to go for the day, in the company of several uncles, aunts and cousins, to an old restaurant called Le Café des Pigeons, on the way to the Pyramids. There we would feast on charcoal-grilled pigeons raised in the neighbourhood.

I cannot recollect a more delicious meal. Huge platters piled high with halved baby pigeons, sprinkled with lemon juice and chopped chervil or parsley, were brought to us in the ancient gardens of the restaurant, overgrown with jasmine and bougainvillaea. We ate them all, even their small soft bones.

Meat Dishes

In Arabic literature and folklore, meat dishes have always been labelled the food of the rich and aristocratic, in contrast to the filling dishes of beans, lentils and wheat which are the diet of the lowly poor. Many stories and proverbs illustrate this distinction.

KOFTA MESHWEYA
Grilled Minced Meat on Skewers

Each country and each area in the Middle East has its favourite flavourings for *kofta*. Here is a basic recipe, giving a few simple alternative seasonings. Use fat meat to keep it moist and juicy. If you find it difficult to put the meat on skewers, make it into burgers.

1 kg (2 lb) lamb, beef or a mixture of both, minced
2 onions, grated
Salt and black pepper
Optional seasonings: 1 teaspoon ground cinnamon, or 1 teaspoon
  allspice, or 1 teaspoon ground cumin and 1 teaspoon
  ground coriander

In the past, meat was put through the mincer two or three times, then pounded to a paste in a mortar. Now you can cut the meat into pieces and turn it to a soft paste in food processor. Add the remaining ingredients and blend again.

Take smallish lumps of the mixture and pat them into sausage shapes around flat and wide metal skewers. If grilling over a barbecue, wait until the charcoal has stopped smoking and glows dull red before you place the skewers over it. Make sure the grid is well oiled to prevent the meat from sticking to it. Turn the skewers until the *koftas* are cooked and browned all over, but still pink and juicy inside.

Serve nestling in warm Arab bread or pitta to catch the juices, or with plain rice, and accompanied by salad.

≈ A very special version of this *kofta* is made with a few pine nuts worked into the meat. It is usually shaped in small ovals around the skewer.

≈ In Turkey they serve *kofta kebab* on a bed of yoghourt beaten with a sprinkling of salt, pepper, chopped parsley and mint, and topped with chopped tomatoes.

≈ You can also spoon a little of the yoghourt on to the meat and garnish with chopped spring onion. This is called *youğrtlu kebab*.

≈ Cook them under a grill and serve them on a bed of parsley or chervil, sprinkled with finely chopped onions, as they do in Egypt.

DALA' MAHSHI
Stuffed Breast of Lamb

This is an exquisite and extremely cheap dish. We serve it at Passover with a pyramid of extra stuffing.

47

It is one of the Middle Eastern fruit and meat dishes inspired by ancient Persia. A quince sauce, stewed apples, black cherry jam or cranberry sauce may be substituted for the apricots in this recipe.

> *2 whole large breasts of lamb*
> *Oil*
> *Salt and black pepper*
> *250 g (8 oz) dried apricots – a sharp kind*
> *1 tablespoon sugar*

> STUFFING
> *500 g (1 lb) long-grain rice*
> *2 medium-sized onions, chopped*
> *2–3 tablespoons oil*
> *250 g (8 oz) beef, minced*
> *3 tablespoons finely chopped flat-leaf parsley*
> *Salt and black pepper*
> *120 g (4 oz) pine nuts or chopped walnuts*
> *120 g (4 oz) small seedless black raisins (optional)*

Ask the butcher to chine the meat and to cut a pouch between the skin and the ribs – or do the latter yourself with a long, sharp knife. Wipe clean with a damp cloth.

Prepare the stuffing. Wash the rice first in very hot and then in cold water, then drain well in a colander. Fry the chopped onions in oil until golden brown in a large saucepan. Add the minced beef and fry until browned. Add the rice and continue to fry for a few minutes until well coated. Sprinkle with parsley and pour in an equal volume of boiling water as you have of rice (i.e. for 2 cups of raw rice add 2 cups water). Season to taste with salt and pepper, cover the pan tightly and simmer undisturbed over low heat for 20 minutes, or until the water has been absorbed and the rice is tender but still firm. Remove from the heat and, when cool, add the nuts and, if you wish, raisins. Sometimes the stuffing is coloured with ½ teaspoon saffron or turmeric, or perfumed with a tablespoon of orange blossom water, but I do not personally care for these additions.

Stuff the pouches with the rice mixture. Rub them with oil, salt and pepper, and roast, uncovered, in an oven preheated to 220°C (425°F/Mark 7), then reduced to 160°C (325°F/Mark 3). Roast for about 1 hour, or until the meat is well cooked and browned on the outside.

Put the apricots in a small saucepan with 1 tablespoon sugar and their soaking water. Bring to the boil and simmer, uncovered, for about 20 minutes. By this time the apricots will be soft and the liquid reduced.

A few minutes before serving, pour off the excess fat from the roasting tin. Turn the oven up to 230°C (450°F/Mark 8). Pour the apricot sauce over the lamb and glaze in the oven for 5 to 7 minutes. Do not leave in the oven too long, as the apricots burn easily.

≈ Instead of being roasted, the lamb may be braised on top of the stove. It is first seared in hot fat to brown it all over, then simmered until quite tender. The apricots and their water are added after searing, and the lamb simmers with them gently for about ¾ to 1 hour. In this method, there is no need to simmer the apricots separately first. They need only be soaked.

ARMENIAN KOFTA

500 g (1 lb) potatoes, boiled and mashed
750 g (1½ lb) lean lamb or veal, minced
1 egg, beaten
Salt and black pepper
30–60 g (1–2 oz) pine nuts
Butter
30–60 g (1–2 oz) small seedless raisins
Flour
Oil for deep-frying

Mix the potatoes and minced meat together in a bowl. Add beaten egg, and salt and pepper to taste, and knead vigorously by hand until the mixture is very smooth and soft. Fry the pine nuts in butter for a minute or two to colour them lightly. Drain and knead them into the meat and potato mixture, together with the raisins.

Shape into walnut-sized balls. Roll them in flour and deep-fry in hot oil until crisp and brown on the outside and well done inside.

DAOUD PASHA
Meat Balls with Pine Nuts and Tomato Sauce

1 kg (2 lb) lamb, beef or veal, minced
Salt and black pepper
Seasonings: 1 teaspoon ground cinnamon or allspice, or
   ¾ teaspoon each ground cumin and coriander
2 largish onions, cut in half-moon slices

Oil
60 g (2 oz) pine nuts
1 medium tin tomato concentrate
Juice of ½ lemon
2 tablespoons finely chopped parsley

Mince, pound and knead the meat to a smooth paste or do this in a food processor. Add salt, pepper and seasoning (I prefer cinnamon for this dish). Knead well and roll into marble-sized balls.

In a saucepan or deep frying-pan, fry the onion slices gently in a little oil or butter until golden and transparent. Add the meat balls and sauté over low heat, shaking the pan and rolling the balls about almost constantly to colour them all over. Add the pine nuts and fry gently for 2 minutes longer. Mix the tomato concentrate with a little water and add it to the pan. Add more water, enough to cover the balls; flavour with lemon juice and season with salt and pepper. Stir well and simmer over low heat until the balls are well done and the sauce is reduced; add more water from time to time if the sauce reduces too quickly.

A few minutes before serving, adjust the seasoning and sprinkle the dish with finely chopped parsley.

≈ An attractive way of serving this dish is to fry extra pine nuts in oil for about 2 minutes until lightly coloured. When the meat balls are cooked, decorate each one by sticking a pine nut into the top. Serve with plain white rice.

≈ A popular variation is to knead the same quantity of pine nuts into the meat ball mixture instead of having them in the sauce.

KIBBEH

Kibbeh is the great love of the inhabitants of the Fertile Crescent. It is the national dish of Syria and Lebanon, and Iraq boasts dozens of *koubba*. There are innumerable versions of this family of dishes which epitomize the food of the area. *Kibbeh* is said to have been mentioned in ancient Assyrian and Sumerian writings and to have been served by King Ashur Nassir Bal II. Today the daily life of the people revolves around its preparation, a dramatic ritual. The pounding of the meat and wheat in a stone or metal mortar with a heavy metal pestle is a sound that wakens one in the morning and lulls one to sleep in the afternoon, a sound instantly provoked by the arrival of an unexpected guest or a ring of the door-bell.

I know of no other dish whose preparation is enveloped by such a mystique. Some women are known to have a special 'hand' or 'finger' for making *kibbeh*. This knack is envied by other women and especially by their husbands. One is said to be favoured by the gods if one is born with a long finger, which makes the shaping of *kibbeh* easier.

Today, one can use a food processor to save all the mincing and pounding, and a machine has recently been developed in the Lebanon which takes care of the whole process.

There are countless variations of *kibbeh*, some widely known throughout the Middle East, others less common or belonging to one particular community.

The most common *kibbeh* is a mixture of fine cracked

wheat or burghul, grated onion and minced lamb pounded to a paste. Eaten raw, it is called *kibbeh nayé*. The same paste can be fried or grilled. In *kibbeh bil sanieh*, a layer of minced meat filling is sandwiched between two layers of *kibbeh* and baked in the oven. Stuffed *kibbeh* are hollow, oval or long torpedo-shaped shells of the same paste, filled with a minced meat mixture and deep-fried.

Small *kibbeh* are often added to aubergine and other vegetable stews, or are cooked in yoghourt, pomegranate juice, or sesame meal mixed with orange juice.

Syrian women stake their reputations on their stuffed *kibbeh*. The art lies in making the outer shells as long (at least that is what we thought in Egypt, for I realize now that the Lebanese prefer a small, oval, stocky shape), as thin and as even as possible. The crisp, light, tasty shells should crack to divulge a juicy, aromatic meat filling.

MEAT STEWS WITH FRUIT

I have found many Moroccan *touajen* (the plural form of *tagine*) incredibly like al-Baghdadi's medieval stews – a mysterious culinary bond between ancient Persia and modern Morocco.

Many Moroccans originate from the regions of the Yemen, Iraq and Saudi Arabia. They came there at different times: first in the pre-Christian era, then with the Arab Islamic invasion in the seventh century, and then again in the twelfth, thirteenth and fourteenth centuries. I suspect that the Arabs of the Abbassid period (the time of al-Baghdadi) brought these dishes with them. They were then spread, Together with Iberian Moorish dishes, throughout a vast Empire by the Moroccan Almoravid and Almohad dynasties, and again during the Sharifian dynasty of the descendants of Fatima, daughter of the Prophet, who came from Arabia at the end of the fourteenth century.

The same fruits – apples, prunes, quinces, apricots and raisins – and to a large extent the same spices, are used by Moroccans today as were used by the ancient Persians and the Arabs of the Abbassid period. Al-Baghdadi's recipes recommend mashing the fruits to a pulp, but Moroccans leave them whole or sliced, and add them towards the end of cooking, to prevent them disintegrating. Fasis (inhabitants of Fez) stew their ingredients, as al-Baghdadi did, without preliminary frying, as they consider that frying would add heaviness to otherwise delicate dishes.

Every Moroccan family prizes its own very special *touajen* which generations of their cooks have prepared for them, keeping the recipes fiercely secret.

MISHMISHIYA

A splendid meat and apricot dish which derives its name from the Arabic word for the fruit, *mishmish*. Lamb seems to have a special affinity for apricots, and a similar dish was a great favourite in our family.

From al-Baghdadi's thirteenth-century cookery manual.

Cut fat meat small, put into the saucepan with a little salt, and cover with water. Boil and remove the scum. Cut up onions, wash, and throw in on top of the meat. Add seasonings, coriander, cummin, mastic, cinnamon, pepper and ginger, well ground. Take dry apricots, soak in hot water, then wash and put in a separate saucepan, and boil lightly: take out, wipe in the hands, and strain through a sieve. Take the juice, and add it to the saucepan to form a broth. Take sweet almonds, grind fine, moisten with a little apricot juice and throw in. Some colour with a trifle of saffron. Spray the saucepan with a little rose-water, wipe its sides with a clean rag, and leave to settle over the fire: then remove.

SUGGESTED QUANTITIES

1 kg (2 lb) shoulder of lamb, cubed, trimmed of excess fat
Salt
1–2 onions, finely chopped
½ teaspoon ground coriander
½ teaspoon ground cumin
¼ teaspoon pulverized mastic (optional)
1–1½ teaspoons ground cinnamon
Black pepper
¼ teaspoon ground ginger
500 g (1 lb) dried apricots, soaked and blended to a purée
60 g (2 oz) ground almonds
¼ teaspoon saffron (optional)
1 teaspoon rose water

The meat is not fried before stewing. It may seem dull at first, but the apricot sauce thickened with the ground almonds gives it a particular richness which makes frying superfluous. The apricots must be of a sharp (not sweet) variety. The stew requires about 2 hours of gentle cooking. Keep adding water. Leave out the mastic and saffron if you wish – I do not think they are at all necessary.

LAHMA BIL KARAZ
Meat Balls with Cherries

A Syrian dish one of my aunts used to make.

> 1 kg (2 lb) lean lamb or veal, minced
> Salt and black pepper
> ½ teaspoon grated nutmeg
> ½ teaspoon ground cloves
> ½ teaspoon ground cinnamon
> Oil
> 500 g (1 lb) morello cherries, pitted, or 250g (8 oz) dried sour
>   cherries
> Sugar and/or lemon juice
> Rounds of Arab bread or pitta

Mince the meat two or three times, then knead vigorously by hand to achieve a smooth, pasty texture, or use
a food processor. Season with the salt, pepper and spices,
and knead again. Form marble-sized balls with the mixture and fry them gently in oil, shaking the pan to colour
them all over.

Fresh, pitted sour cherries or dried ones should be
used for this dish if possible. If these are not available,
use tinned ones. Stew the fresh cherries in a large pan
with a very little water, adding sugar and/or lemon juice
to taste according to the sweetness or acidity of the fruit.
Soak dried cherries overnight. If using tinned fruit, add
only lemon as they will be sweet enough already. Add
the sautéed meat balls, and simmer gently until cooked
through, crushing the cherries with a fork when they

become soft enough. Let the sugar in the sauce become caramelized a little, but add more water if this happens before the meat balls are cooked and the fruit is soft.

This dish is traditionally served on opened art Arab bread, soft side up. If this is not available, cut thinnish slices of white bread, remove the crusts and arrange the slices on a large serving dish. Cover each slice with several meat balls and some cherry sauce. Served in this manner, they can be picked up and eaten like an open sandwich.

≈ A richer variation involves preparing a tomato sauce with a chopped onion fried with a clove of garlic, some skinned and chopped tomatoes, a little tomato concentrate and water. The cherries and meat balls are added to this sauce and simmered in it until tender.

MOROCCAN TAGINE WITH PRUNES

This fragrant dish, a speciality of Fez, can be prepared with various fruits – apples, pears or quinces, for example, instead of prunes. This version using prunes is a Moroccan favourite, particularly good as a winter dish. Honey is sometimes added, its sweetness sometimes threatened with a little ginger and much pepper. Saffron is traditionally added, but its taste is almost lost among the rich flavours and its high cost therefore makes it, in my opinion, optional.

1 kg (2 lb) shoulder of lamb, cubed, trimmed of excess fat
2–3 tablespoons oil
¼ teaspoon ground ginger

¼ teaspoon saffron (optional)
Salt and black pepper
½ teaspoon ground coriander
1 teaspoon ground cinnamon
1 onion, finely chopped
250 g (8 oz) prunes, soaked overnight
1–2 tablespoons honey, or to taste (optional)
1 teaspoon orange blossom water
Roasted or grilled sesame seeds, to garnish (optional)

Put the meat in a large saucepan, cover with water and add oil, ginger, saffron if used, salt and pepper to taste, coriander, cinnamon and the finely chopped onion. Bring to the boil, cover the pan and simmer very gently until the meat is tender and the water has become a rich sauce, adding water to keep the meat covered and reducing the sauce at the end. This will take about 2 hours.

Add the prunes and simmer for 20 minutes longer. Stir the honey into the sauce, blending it in well, and cook for a further 15 minutes. Sprinkle with orange blossom water. The dish is sometimes served garnished with roasted or grilled sesame seeds.

Substantial Dishes

Since ancient times, dishes based on chick peas, beans, lentils and cereals have been looked down on as the food of the poor. In literature, proverbs and songs they are constantly referred to as 'the food of the poor' or 'the food of the mean'. They have even been included as such in the *Kitab al Buhala* (*Book of Misers*).*

Regardless of this stigma, these dishes are nevertheless loved by rich and poor alike.

A number of Arab dishes go under the name of fatta, which describes the manner of breaking crisp bread into pieces with your hands. They all have a bed of toasted bread soaked in flavoursome stock and a topping of yoghourt with a variety of fillings. The most common filling is chick peas.

FATTET HUMMUS
Chick Peas with Yoghourt and Toasted Bread

90–120 g (3–4 oz) chick peas, soaked overnight
Salt
½ litre (1 pint) yoghourt
3 cloves garlic, crushed
Pepper

* By Jahiz, Damascus, 1938.

2 *pitta breads*
Oil for frying (optional)
1–2 tablespoons crushed dried mint leaves
3 tablespoons pine nuts or slivered almonds
1 tablespoon butter (or clarified butter)

Drain the chick peas and simmer in fresh water to cover until they are very tender, usually well over an hour, adding salt only when they are nearly done. Drain the yoghourt in a muslin cloth placed in a sieve for about ¾ hour, until it is the thickness of mayonnaise. Alternatively use a ½ and ½ mix of natural yoghurt and thick Greek-style yoghurt. Then pour into a bowl and beat in the garlic and salt and pepper to taste. Open out the bread and toast it in a very hot oven until it is crisp and brown. Then break it up into the bottom of the serving dish. Alternatively, cut the bread into triangles and deep fry in hot oil, then drain on absorbent paper. Pour the chick peas and some of their water over the bread, soaking it thoroughly, keeping a few to decorate the dish. Pour the yoghourt mixture over the chick peas and sprinkle with mint.

To garnish, fry the pine nuts or almonds in sizzling butter until they are a light brown and sprinkle over the yoghourt with the extra chick peas. Serve at once with the chick peas hot and the rest lukewarm.

≈ This is often served for breakfast with tea, accompanied by whole spring onions and green peppers cut into strips. Some people like to sprinkle it with hot red chilli pepper or cayenne.

≈ A Damascus version called *tasseia* has the chick peas crushed with a pestle and mortar and mixed with 4 or 5 tablespoons of tahina, the juice of ½ lemon and 1 crushed clove of garlic. You can put it in a blender with a little of the cooking liquor. Squeeze a little lemon juice in the chick pea water before sprinkling over the bread, spread the mashed chick pea cream over the top and cover with yoghourt, then garnish as before.

FUL MEDAMES
Egyptian Brown Beans

An Egyptian dish which has become 'the' national dish. *Ful medames* is pre-Ottoman and pre-Islamic, claimed by the Copts and probably as old as the Pharaohs. According to an Arab saying: 'Beans have satisfied even the Pharaohs.'

Although basically a peasant dish, the rich and the middle classes also delight in these small dark beans.

Ful medames is eaten in the fields and in village mud houses, in luxury restaurants and on town terraces by masters and servants alike. It is sold in the streets, sometimes buried in Arab bread garnished with tahina salad and accompanied by a tomato and onion salad. It is the usual substantial breakfast traditionally cooked overnight in an earthen vessel buried up to the neck in ashes.

1 kg (2 lb) Egyptian brown beans, soaked overnight
2–4 cloves garlic, crushed (to taste)
Finely chopped flat-leaf parsley
Olive oil

Quartered lemons
Salt and freshly ground black pepper
1 teaspoon cumin (optional)

Boil the drained beans in a fresh portion of unsalted water in a large saucepan until tender. In the past this took at least 7 hours but the qualities available now are soft after 2 to 2½ hours of gentle simmering. A pressure cooker will reduce the time considerably – to 30 or 45 minutes – but care must be taken not to overcook the beans.

When the beans are soft and the liquid reduced, serve them and add crushed garlic to taste, or pass it round with the other garnishes for people to take as much as they want.

Serve in soup bowls and sprinkle with chopped parsley. Pass round olive oil, quartered lemons, salt, black pepper and cumin for each person to season as they wish.

≈ It is common to serve a hard-boiled egg on top of each serving of the beans.
≈ A pleasant way of thickening the sauce is to throw a handful of red lentils into the water at the start of the cooking.
≈ In Iraq large brown beans are used instead of the small Egyptian ones in a dish called *badkila*, which also serves for breakfast in the street.
≈ Another way of serving *ful medames* is to smother it in a tomato sauce flavoured with garlic.
≈ Yet another is to top it with a chopped mixed salad and thinly sliced onions or spring onions.

MEGADARRA

Here is a modern version of a medieval dish called *muja-darra*, described by al-Baghdadi as a dish of the poor, and still known today as Esau's favourite. In fact, it is such a great favourite that although said to be for misers, it is a compliment to serve it.

An aunt of mine used to present it regularly to guests with the comment: 'Excuse the food of the poor!' – to which the unanimous reply always was: 'Keep your food of kings and give us *megadarra* every day!'

The proportions of lentils and rice vary with every family. The caramelized onions are the main feature. With the olive oil they are also the main flavouring. In the Lebanon they call it *mudardara*.

250 g (8 oz) large brown lentils
2 onions, finely chopped
125 ml (4 fl oz) olive oil
Salt and black pepper
250 g (8 oz) long-grain rice, washed
2–3 onions, sliced into half-moon shapes

Wash and drain the lentils. Boil in a fresh portion of water to cover for about 25 minutes or until only just tender. Fry the chopped onions in 2 to 3 tablespoons oil until they are brown. Add them to the lentils and season to taste with salt and pepper. Mix well and add rice, together with enough water to make the liquid in the pan up to the volume of rice. Season again and simmer gently, covered, for about 20 minutes until the rice is soft and well cooked, adding a little more water if it becomes absorbed too quickly.

Fry the sliced onions in the rest of the very hot oil until they are dark brown and sweet, almost caramelized.

Serve the rice and lentils on a large shallow dish, garnished with the fried onion slices and their oil poured over.

This dish is delicious served warm or at room temperature, and accompanied by yoghourt.

≈ A tip: you may find it easier to cook rice and lentils separately and to mix them together when they are both done.

≈ For different flavours add 1 teaspoon cumin and 1 teaspoon coriander in the cooking water or 2 teaspoons dried mint.

≈ In another dish of rice and lentils called *masafi*, the lentils are turned to a purée. Red lentils, which disintegrate easily, can be used for this.

COUSCOUS

Couscous is the national dish of the Maghreb, the North African countries of Morocco, Tunisia and Algeria. Of Berber origin, this is a truly local dish. A couscous has been adopted by other Arab countries, who call it *maghrebia*, but this is very different from the one eaten in North Africa.

Couscous itself is a type of fine semolina made from durum hard wheat. Until very recently, every family would send its wheat (bought at the market) to the local mill to be ground to the degree of fineness they preferred. Back home, the grain went through a process of rubbing with fine flour. It was put in a large wooden bowl and moistened with a little water. Gradually, flour was sprinkled over it, while the women rolled it into the couscous with their hands so as to coat each grain with a fine film of flour. This was in order to keep each grain separate when it was steamed. Today, most people buy their couscous ready prepared for the sake of expediency.

There are infinite regional and family variations of the dish. Every time it is made it is different, the women putting all their expertise into varying it and yet keeping to the traditional form.

The traditional process for the cooking of couscous is the steaming of the grain over a broth. This is generally made with meat, usually lamb or chicken, and a variety of vegetables. Chick peas are usually added, and sometimes raisins as well. The broth is often coloured red with tomato purée or yellow with saffron. Many spices are used but so sparingly that one can hardly define each individual aroma. Often a sauce is prepared separately with some of the broth and made strong and fiery with cayenne or chilli pepper or a red pepper paste called *harissa* (see page 9). This sauce is served beside the couscous for those who wish to be 'inflamed and intoxicated'.

In the Moroccan city of Fez, the broths are generally lighter. The ingredients are boiled and delicately perfumed.

In Tunisia and Algeria, they are richer and heavier. The meat, and sometimes the vegetables as well, is first braised in oil. Tunisians prefer spicier broths with cayenne and chilli. Algerians like to add tomato purée, while Moroccans prefer the aroma and colour given by a pinch of saffron.

MOROCCAN COUSCOUS

Here is a basic Moroccan couscous around which you can improvise.

The commercial varieties of couscous we get in boxes in Britain are pre-cooked and instant (they are 'medium' size granules) and only need the same volume of water to be added before heating through.

1 kg (2 lb) lean stewing lamb or 500 g (1 lb) lamb, 250 g
    (8 oz) beef and ½ chicken
2 onions, chopped
60 g (2 oz) chick peas, soaked overnight
2 turnips, quartered
2 large carrots, sliced
2 tablespoons olive oil
Salt and black pepper
¼ teaspoon ground ginger (optional)
¼ teaspoon saffron (optional)
500 g (1 lb) or more couscous
60–120 g (2–4 oz) raisins
3 courgettes, sliced, or ½ marrow, cut in pieces
120 g (4 oz) fresh shelled or frozen broad beans
2 tomatoes
A bunch flat-leaf parsley, finely chopped
A bunch coriander, finely chopped
Cayenne or chilli pepper
1 teaspoon paprika
3 tablespoons butter

Put the meat, chicken if used, onions, chick peas, turnips

and carrots – all the ingredients which require longer cooking – in the bottom part of a large pan. Cover with water, add the oil and pepper, and ginger and saffron if you like, bring to the boil and simmer for about 1 hour. Add salt only when the chick peas have softened.

Add raisins, courgettes or marrow, broad beans, tomatoes, parsley and coriander to the simmering broth. Cook for a further ½ hour.

In the meantime prepare the grain. Put the couscous in a wide oven dish in which you can serve. Gradually add the same volume of warm salted water (with ½–1 teaspoon of salt), stirring all the time so that it is absorbed evenly. Keep fluffing up the grain with a fork and breaking up any lumps. After about 10–15 minutes, when the grain is plump and tender, mix in 3 tablespoons of vegetable oil and rub the grain between your hands above the bowl to air it and break up any lumps. Put the dish, uncovered, in a preheated 200°C (400°F/Mark 6) oven to heat through for 20 minutes until very hot. Before serving, work in the butter and break up any lumps very thoroughly.

Take a good cupful of sauce from the stew and stir in cayenne or chilli pepper, enough to make it very strong and fiery, and a little paprika.

Arrange the meat and vegetables over the couscous and pour the broth over it. Pass the hot, peppery sauce round separately in a little bowl.

Alternatively, serve the couscous, the meat and vegetables, the broth and the peppery sauce in separate bowls.

Stuffed Vegetables

Dolma to the Turks, *dolmathes* to the Greeks, *dolmeh* to the Iranians, and *mahshi* to the Arabs, stuffed vegetables are the great family favourites, the party pieces and festive dishes of the Turks, the Uzbeks, the Azerbaijanis, Armenians, Greeks, Egyptians, Iranians, Syrians, Lebanese, Saudi Arabians and North Africans. Adopted by all, each country has developed its own variations.

Their origin is not certain, though both the Turks and the Greeks claim them as their creation. They do not appear in the very early Persian and Arab manuscripts, but seem to have been known at the time of the Ottoman Empire, and were served at the lavish banquets of the Sultans. Perhaps they were developed at this time; but they may equally well have been adopted from the vanquished Greeks, who claim a rich culinary tradition stemming from their early civilization.

However, stuffed vegetables were obviously developed as a 'court cuisine', invented and prepared for a rich and powerful leisured class to excite their curiosity and titillate their palates, as well as to satisfy their desire for ostentation. The long, elaborate preparation required for these dishes, and the experienced and delicate handiwork that goes into the making of them are proof of the number of dedicated cooks employed in the huge kitchens, while the subtle harmony of the vegetables and their fillings demonstrates the refined taste and deep culinary knowledge of their masters.

Today, poorer people can usually afford vine leaves, courgettes, onions and aubergines; and although they have had to make the fillings simpler and cheaper, they count their own time as cheap, and spend it lavishly on rolling and filling their beloved *mahshi*.

As well as the love for different, subtle flavours, for the exciting fusion of vegetables and their fillings, the traditional wish to take pains and give of oneself is satisfied by the trouble one takes in making these dishes. So is the wish to impress by one's culinary expertise. And how the guest loves to be surprised by an intriguing parcel, the contents of which are always slightly unpredictable!

In the past, Arabs have been – and in certain places still are – obsessed by their belief in the existence of numerous spirits or *djinns*, several *djinns* per person in fact, who inhabit both things and people whenever they get a chance. Their tales give a fascinating picture of vegetables inhabited by *djinns* – rice *djinns*, meat *djinns*, chick pea *djinns* – seasoned and spiced, and given piquant, naughty or gentle personalities, like the *djinns* who inhabit humans.

A very common filling for any stuffed vegetable is a mixture of chopped onion, minced meat, rice and chopped parsley, sometimes with chopped tomatoes as well, seasoned with salt and pepper. Sometimes raisins, pine nuts and chopped walnuts are added to the mixture. Iranians favour the addition of well-cooked yellow split peas. An Armenian filling is made with burghul (cracked wheat) flavoured with aniseed and garlic.

In the past, stuffed vegetables were customarily fried

gently in oil or *samna* (clarified butter) before being stewed. Today, since the tendency is to make dishes lighter and less rich, this step, though an enhancement to the flavour of the dish, is omitted.

Almost any vegetable can be, and is, stuffed.

IMAM BAYILDI
Cold Stuffed Aubergines with Onions and Tomatoes

This famous Turkish dish is served as a cold appetizer or first course. Conflicting stories are told about the origin of its name which means 'the imam fainted'. Some say it came about when an *imam* (Muslim priest) fainted with pleasure on being served it by his wife. Others believe that the *imam* fainted when he heard how expensive the ingredients were, and how much olive oil had gone into the making. The dish can be cooked in a saucepan or in the oven.

6 small, thin aubergines
Salt
80 ml (3 fl oz) extra virgin olive oil
250 ml (9 fl oz) good-quality tomato juice
1 teaspoon sugar, or more
Juice of 1 lemon

FOR THE FILLING

1½ large onions, cut in ½ and sliced thinly
2–3 tablespoons extra virgin olive oil
5 garlic cloves, chopped
1 cup chopped flat-leaf parsley

70

4 tomatoes, skinned and chopped
Salt

Trim the stalk ends of the aubergines (you may keep the stalk). Peel off ½ inch wide strips of skin lengthways leaving alternate strips of peel and bare flesh. Make a deep cut on one side of each aubergine lengthways, from one end to the other, but not right through, so as to make a pocket.

For the filling, soften the onions gently in the oil in a frying pan, but do not let them colour. Add garlic and stir for a moment or two until the aroma rises. Remove from the heat and stir in the parsley and tomatoes. Add salt to taste and mix well.

Stuff the aubergines with this mixture and place them tightly side by side, with the opening on top, in a wide shallow pan. Pour over them the oil and enough tomato juice to cover, mixed with a little sugar, salt, and the lemon juice. Cover the pan and simmer gently for about 45 minutes or until the aubergines are very soft and the liquid much reduced. Allow to cool before transferring to a serving dish. Serve cold.

≈ A variation is to bake the aubergines. Arrange them in a baking dish, cut side on top, with the rest of the ingredients poured over. Cover with foil and cook in a preheated 200°C (400°F/gas 6) oven for 1 hour or until soft.

ONIONS STUFFED WITH MEAT

3 large onions
750 g (1½ lb) minced beef
A few sprigs of flat-leaf parsley, finely chopped

Salt and pepper
1½ teaspoons cinnamon
½ teaspoon allspice
1–2 tablespoons tamarind paste
1 tablespoon sugar
3 tablespoons oil

Peel the onions and cut off the ends. With a sharp knife make a cut from top to bottom on one side of each onion through to the centre. Throw into boiling water and cook until the onions soften and start to open so that each layer can be detached (about 15 minutes). Drain and cool, then separate each layer carefully.

Make the filling by working the minced meat with the parsley, salt and pepper, cinnamon and allspice. Put a small lump into each onion layer and roll up tightly.

Line the bottom of a heavy pan with the discarded bits of onion. Pack the stuffed onion rolls closely over them.

Cover with water (about 150 ml/¼ pint) in which you have dissolved the tamarind paste and sugar and added the oil. Place a small plate on top and simmer gently, adding a little water if necessary, until they are very soft and the water mainly absorbed. Serve hot or cold.

≈ You may like to arrange the onions on a heatproof dish after cooking, sprinkle with a little extra sugar and let them caramelize under the grill.

SWEET-AND-SOUR DISHES

Reading quite recently about ancient pre-Islamic Persia of the Sassanid period and its Zoroastrian dualist religion, which is based on the confrontation of the two enemy forces of good and evil, I was struck by the similarity between the early philosophy of the Persians and principles of harmony which they apply to their food.

The Zoroastrian belief is that their god Ahouramazda created the world. The spirit of creation which pulled matter out of nothing awoke a force of resistance, giving birth to a spirit of evil, Angromainyous, whose creative and malicious urge was to destroy the harmony of the universe. In this religion, creation could only exist in the equilibrium of the opposing forces which it had aroused.

It is this same equilibrium, poised between the vinegar and the sugar, the quince and the meat, which the Persians of the Sassanid period reflected in their dishes. Both ancient and modern Persian dishes blend opposite flavours and textures, coupling sweet with sour or spicy, strong with mild. These dishes were adopted by the Caliphs of Baghdad, and some were taken further afield to Morocco. (Some Middle Eastern countries have not, however, adopted the more markedly sweet-and-sour dishes, although welcoming most others.)

During the same period, parts of India adopted a version of the Zoroastrian religion – the Parsees of today, but with one god of creation, and without a necessary enemy or evil force. North Indian food is not unlike Persian food, but, strangely, it seems to lack the particular harmony through opposites which the Persian dishes have.

It is also interesting to compare the Middle Eastern 'sweet and sour' with that of China. The Chinese have a

73

predilection for sweet and sour, and harmony through opposites, and their early religion was one also based on opposing forces of good and evil.

LEEKS WITH LEMON AND SUGAR

This is a particularly delicious sweet-and-sour way of preparing leeks

1 kg (2 lb) leeks
2–3 cloves garlic, crushed
1 tablespoon sugar
3–4 tablespoons sunflower oil
Juice of 1 lemon

Wash the leeks carefully, removing any soil nestling between the leaves. Cut off the tough green part of the leaves. Cut the rest into medium pieces.

Fry the garlic and sugar in hot oil until they just begin to colour. Add the leeks and turn them a little over moderate heat. Sprinkle with lemon juice. Add ½ teacup of water and stew gently, covered, over very low heat until soft.

Serve hot or cold.

Rice

RICE

While wheat is the staple of the rural parts of the Middle East, rice is the everyday food of the cities. It was introduced in the marshlands of the area through Persia from India. It is often the main part of the meal, with small amounts of meat and vegetables acting as garnish or accompaniment. It is *roz* to the Arabs, *pirinç*, or pilav when cooked with other ingredients, to the Turks. Iranians call it *chilau* when it is plain, and *polo* when cooked with other ingredients. In the Arabian Gulf they have taken to an Indian way of making it called *birian*.

Cooked plainly with water, salt and a little oil or butter, it serves as an accompaniment to stews or grilled meats and salads, or is itself accompanied by rich sauces. It can also be cooked together with other ingredients, added to the sauce of a meat stew when the meat is already tender, or partially cooked and added to other cooked ingredients to finish cooking together.

Rice is sometimes coloured yellow with saffron or turmeric, or red with tomatoes. It is moulded into various shapes, the favourite one being a ring, and often garnished with nuts and sauces.

HOW TO COOK RICE

Throughout the Middle East, the preparation of rice is enveloped by a certain ritual mystique. Although an extremely simple dish, various ways of cooking it exist. Each family cherishes a particular method and is sceptical about all others, refusing to believe that it is possible to achieve successful results in any way other than their own. Generally speaking however, each country seems to prefer one method above all others. I have given those most commonly followed.

Long-grain rice is used except for stuffing vegetables, when short- or medium-grain rice is preferred because it sticks together. The particular qualities of the longer grain lie in its fluffiness, and its ability to remain firm and separate. If well cooked, it is tender but firm, not too soft, and never mushy. Varieties of long-grain rice available in Britain include *basmati* and *patna* rice from India, and the American 'Uncle Ben'.

Basically, plain rice is cooked in water with salt and some fat – usually butter, clarified butter or oil. The quantity of water necessary and the cooking times vary. Each batch of rice is different and so, as households buy it by the large sackful, the first dish made from the opened sack ascertains the amount of water and the time required for cooking the rest. Generally the same volume of water as that of dry raw rice is needed, but if the rice is a year old more water must be used. It also depends on the type of grain.

The rice is almost always cooked in a pan with a

tightly fitting lid, but a few people prefer to leave the lid only half on. In this case, more water must be used to make up for the rapid evaporation.

When rice comes in hessian sacks it has to be cleaned of stones and roughage (and sometimes small insects too) and washed many times before it is ready for cooking. The pre-packed rice available is perfectly clean and needs only to be rid of the starchy powder which causes it to be less separate and slightly sticky when cooked. Some people do not object to this and find the result of rice cooked without preliminary washing very acceptable, maintaining that the zeal of excessive washing is a hangover from the 'hessian sack' era.

A special word about Persian rice. As with her art of miniature painting and poetry, Persia has carried the preparation of rice to extraordinary heights of refinement. It is a base or accompaniment for practically every dish and it is said that no other Middle Eastern country prepares rice in the same perfectionist manner. Its preparation is often started a day before it is to be eaten.

At least six different qualities of rice are cultivated in Persia. The best, 'royal' rice, called *domsiah*, grows in rare conditions and is very expensive. The next best is *darbori* rice; then come *sadri* and *champâ*. These are not available in Britain. *Basmati* rice is the nearest to the third quality of rice and the best substitute to use.

SABZI POLO
Rice with Fresh Herbs

Iranians have a predilection for fresh herbs. A traditional New Year's dish consists of rice cooked with a variety of fresh herbs; their greenness is believed to ensure a happy and 'green' year ahead.

The herbs are chosen according to individual taste and mood, and to what is available at that time of year. Favourite Iranian herbs include *tare* (tarragon), chives, parsley and dill, and others, including fresh fenugreek and *gishnise*, which I have not found in Britain. Use whichever you prefer, but try to use fresh ones.

Wash and chop the herbs finely. Wash and drain 500 g (1 lb) *basmati* rice. Boil it vigorously in plenty of salted water, and when it is nearly cooked, throw in the herbs. As soon as the rice is tender but not too soft drain in a sieve or colander. The herbs will cling to the rice. Return to the pan, stir in 4 tablespoons of butter, cover with a lid and a cloth stretched under the lid, and steam over very low heat for about 20 minutes.

PERSIAN LAMB AND APRICOT POLO

The apricot has a special affinity for lamb. But it must be of the sharp variety. The early Abbasid dynasty, centred in Baghdad, which was influenced by Persian culture, greatly favoured the combination and created a series of dishes on this theme which they called *mishmishiya*, *mishmish* being the Arab word for apricot. It is still a great favourite as a partner to lamb in modern Iran.

120 g (4 oz) butter
1 onion, finely chopped
500 g (1 lb) lean lamb, cubed
Salt and black pepper

½ teaspoon ground cinnamon
2 tablespoons seedless raisins
120 g (4 oz) sharp dried apricots
2 teacups (500 g/1 lb) basmati rice

Heat 60 g (2 oz) butter in a large, heavy saucepan and fry the onion until soft and golden. Add the meat and fry gently, turning the pieces to brown them all over. Season with salt, pepper and cinnamon. Add raisins and halved apricots, and sauté lightly. Cover with water and simmer gently, covered, for about 1½ hours, until the meat is very tender and has absorbed the sweet and acid flavours of the fruit. If the stew is still rather liquid by the end of cooking time, reduce it by fast boiling.

Wash and drain the rice then boil in salted water for 10–15 minutes until ½ cooked; then drain and mix in the remaining 60 g (2 oz) butter.

Arrange alternate layers of rice and meat with sauce in a non-stick saucepan, starting and ending with a layer of rice. Cover and steam gently for 20–30 minutes longer, until the rice is tender and has absorbed some of the sauce. Turn out like a cake.

SPICED RICE WITH PINE NUTS, PISTACHIOS AND ALMONDS

This is an elegant and decorative way of serving rice at a party. This ring shape is traditional for rice and here it is crowned by an assortment of nuts.

500 g (1 lb) basmati or long-grain rice, washed if necessary
900 ml (1½ pints) chicken stock (you may use a stock cube)

1 teaspoon cardamom seeds (Indian stores sell them out of
   the pod)

6 cloves

3 cinnamon sticks about 3 inches long

Salt and pepper

5 tablespoons butter or vegetable oil plus another tablespoon
   of oil

80 g (3 oz) mixed pistachios and blanched almonds, coarsely
   chopped

80 g (3 oz) pine nuts

Bring the stock to the boil with the cardamom seeds, cloves
and cinnamon sticks and simmer for 10 minutes. Add a
little salt and pepper and pour in the rice. Let it come to the
boil again and stir well, then lower the heat and cook on
very low heat, with the lid, on for about 20 minutes, until
little holes appear on the surface and the rice is tender. Stir
in the 5 tablespoons of butter, cut into pieces, or the oil.

Fry the pistachios and blanched almonds with the
pine nuts in the remaining oil until just beginning to
colour. Spread them evenly over the bottom of an oiled
ring mould large enough to hold all the rice and pack
the rice firmly over the nuts.

Heat through in a medium oven and unmould just
before serving.

ADDAS POLO
Rice with Lentils and Dates

This exquisite and elegant Persian rice can be made with
chicken instead of meat.

500 g basmati rice

1 onion, chopped

100 g (¼lb) butter or 80 ml (3 fl oz) vegetable oil

500 g (1 lb) lamb or beef cut into cubes

Salt and pepper

1 teaspoon cinnamon

¼ teaspoon allspice

180 g (6 oz) brown or green lentils, rinsed

½ teaspoon good quality saffron powder or crushed saffron
  threads soaked in 4 tablespoons hot water

75 g (3 oz) raisins or sultanas, soaked in water for
  15 minutes)

8 pitted semi-dried dates, split in half or coarsely chopped

Wash and drain the rice. Heat 2 tablespoons of the butter or oil in a large frying pan, and fry the onion until golden. Add the meat and sauté, stirring and turning the pieces, until browned all over. Cover with water, add salt and pepper, cinnamon and allspice, and simmer covered for 1 hour or until the meat is very tender and the liquid absorbed.

Boil the lentils in salted water for about 20 minutes, until done, adding salt when they begin to soften. Then drain. Boil the rice in salted water for 10 minutes until not quite tender, and drain. Melt 2 tablespoons of butter at the bottom of a non-stick pan and stir in 2 tablespoons of the saffron and water and about a third of the rice.

Spread ½ the meat on top, then sprinkle on ½ the lentils, raisins and dates. Cover with a layer of rice and the remaining meat, lentils, raisins and dates and finish with the rice that is left. Melt the remaining butter, stir in the remaining saffron and water and pour all over. Cook, covered, on very low heat for 20–30 minutes until the rice is done.

Serve hot. The crisp brown bottom of the rice is a choice bit. You can turn out the rice upside down. If you are using a non-stick pan it will look like a cake with a golden crust.

Bread

In the Middle East, as in the rest of the world, bread is the staff of life. There are many types of bread, leavened and unleavened, thick and paper-thin, which are normally baked over a metal dome on an open fire or in a charcoal oven. The most common is round, flat and only slightly leavened, with a hollow like an empty pocket running right through it. It is made with various qualities of wheat flour: a coarse flour makes an earthy, dark bread, a refined white one results in a delicate white bread. It is soft. Even the outer crust is not crisp but soft, while the inside is chewy, and good for absorbing sauces.

The religious and superstitious feeling attached to bread is stronger in some Middle Eastern countries than others. To some it is, more than any other food, a direct gift from God. A hungry man will kiss a piece of bread given to him as alms. An invocation to God is murmured before kneading the dough, another before placing it in the oven. A piece of bread found lying on the floor is immediately picked up and respectfully placed on the table.

Although bread is available everywhere in towns, many people still prefer to make their own and send it to be baked in the oven of the local bakery, as is done in the villages. Children rushing through the streets balancing a large wooden tray or a flat wicker basket on their heads are a common daily sight. The trays hold rounds of flattened dough laid on a cloth, and covered by another cloth. At the bakery, the children stand close to the big oven, watching where their bread is put down so as not to lose it among the other loaves. People often mark their loaves with a pinch or brand it with a sign drawn with a stick in order to be able to recognize and claim their own when it comes out of the oven.

Bread, often pitta bread, is eaten with every meal. Sometimes people break off a piece and double it over to enclose and pick up a morsel of meat or vegetable, or dip it in a sauce or cream salad, holding it delicately between the thumb and the first two fingers. Sometimes it is cut in half and the pocket is filled with hot shish kebab and salads or *ful medames*. It can also be toasted, or broken into pieces and used as a base for soups, salads and a few stews. Some people, my father among them, claim that they cannot truly savour sauces or juices, or anything in fact, without a piece of bread.

Puddings and Drinks

In the Middle East the usual conclusion to a meal is a bowl of fruit. The sweet pastries, desserts, jams and preserves which have given the region its reputation for a sweet tooth are made to mark special occasions and for entertaining guests. They are symbols of generosity and friendship, happiness, rejoicing and success. Quantities are made regularly and stored away, ready for the casual caller and the unexpected friend, who by Middle Eastern convention, expects and enjoys a warm, enthusiastic welcome at any time of the day. He will invariably be received, even at an awkward time, with the famous Oriental hospitality, the ingrained courtesy and decorum which have been rooted deeply by centuries of custom. Pastries, jams and preserves will be pressed upon him with a Turkish coffee.

Besides spontaneous calls, there are special occasions when visiting is obligatory. A new arrival in town, a return home from a trip, a sickness, a death, a birth, a circumcision, a wedding, and the innumerable Muslim festivals, the *mûlids*, all set the cake- and pastry-making and eating rituals in motion. Certain occasions call for a particular sweet. Pastries, jams and preserves, sweet-scented creams and delicately fragrant dried-fruit salads are made days in advance and served to commemorate or celebrate an event, as symbols of joy or sadness. They are often beautifully coloured and decorated.

Muslim festivals always seem to be in progress. They sometimes last for as long as ten days – ten days of continuous merry-making. Nearly every week brings some excitement and has some saint to be honoured, some memory to be cherished or some rite to be performed. The first ten days of the sacred Moharram, the opening month of the year, are holy. The passion play of Hasan and Hussein follows, performed in reverence to the memory of the martyr Hoseyn. In the second month, caravans of pilgrims returning from Mecca are welcomed with a picnic celebration. In the third month comes the Rabi el Awal or Mûlid el Nabi, the festival of the Prophet's birth. Then come the Mûlid el Bulak, the feast of the Lady Zeinab and the feast of the 'miraculous ascent', the visit to Paradise. After the great fast of Ramadan follow the Id es-Saghir and the visiting of cemeteries. Then there is the procession of Kisweh, of the Holy Carpet, and that of the Mahmal, the Ark of the Covenant.

In Egypt, many of the festivals are not based on either the Muhammadan or the Coptic religions, but derive from ancient Egyptian pagan rites and customs. People want to enjoy themselves and any occasion is a pretext for fun, for laughter and merry-making, for dancing and singing in the streets, for glass- and fire-eating, for *kara Guz* (the Egyptian Punch and Judy), and for tying coloured papers to bicycle spokes. It is a time for putting on dresses in fabulous *baladi* colours – sugar pinks and oranges, mauves, purples, lilacs, limes, acid greens and scarlets – and for wearing Western pyjamas in the streets. It is also a time for buying, from the street vendors, brilliantly coloured violet, pink and pale green syrups, and sweet pastries made with nuts, honey and sugar, and coloured yellow, pink and green, the colours of joy and happiness.

At one particular festival, the day of the sacrifice of the bride of the Nile (the Bent el Nil), we used to buy a large sugar doll painted in many different colours, with red lips and pink cheeks, and dressed in frilled and pleated multi-coloured tissue and silver papers. To my mother's horror, I once ate the whole doll, licking and chewing it for a month, undressing it and dressing it again after every repast.

For me, sweets are particularly associated with feelings of well-being, warmth and welcome, of giving and receiving, of crowds of people smiling, kissing, hugging and showering hospitality. I remember how hard it was to refuse, when visiting our many relatives and friends, the delicacies and pastries that were literally forced upon us, after our mother had impressed on us that we should not take more than three stuffed vine leaves, two *kahk* and two *ma'amoul* because it was discourteous to be too eager and it would appear that we were not properly fed at home. We learnt to say 'No' a few times before we accepted and even today, after many years in Europe, I find it hard to say 'Yes' the first time when offered a drink or something to eat, and then sadly regret the loss of a longed-for tea or pastry.

Many of the pastries are sold in shops which are famous for their specialities. They are also made at home. Every housewife prides herself on making a perfect *konafa* or the lightest *fila*, and will rarely divulge her secrets of success to anyone but her daughter. Or she *may* give the recipe under pressure, but with one deliberate mistake, so as to ensure failure when a competitor attempts it.

It is customary during periods of general festivity for every housewife to prepare mountains of assorted pastries on large trays, to be sent to all her relatives. She duly receives as many in return. On family occasions, relatives and friends come to help the hostess prepare a great variety of dishes days before the party. Sometimes a specialist is called in, a cook who comes to make one or two dishes for which she is famous, and then moves on to another house to make the same dish again. We always knew beforehand if we were to be served Rachèle's *ataïf* or Nabiha's *karabij* or *konafa à la crème*, and we could rejoice for a few days in advance at the thought.

Ever since my parents joined us in Europe, we have been making these specialities ourselves, and we have found them extremely easy to prepare. I am sure that everybody who tries will be able to make them successfully, so I have included them in this chapter with all the old, traditional family sweets.

MUHALLABIA

This most common of Middle Eastern desserts can be quite regal when properly made. It is a milk cream thickened by cornflour or ground rice (in the old days this was pulverized with a pestle and mortar). I have used a mixture of both.

2–3 tablespoons *cornflour*

60 g (2 oz) *ground rice*

A generous litre (2 pints) milk

90 g (3 oz) *sugar, or to taste*

2–3 tablespoons *orange blossom or rose water, or a mixture of
the two*

Chopped almonds and pistachio nuts, to decorate

Mix the cornflour and ground rice to a smooth paste
with a little of the cold milk. Bring the rest of the milk to
the boil and add the paste gradually, stirring constantly
with a wooden spoon. Simmer the mixture gently, stirring constantly but being careful not to scrape the
bottom of the pan (the milk may burn slightly at the bottom and if it is scraped it will give a burnt taste to the
whole pudding). When you feel a slight resistance to the
spoon while stirring, and the mixture coats the back of
the spoon, stir in the sugar and when it thickens a little
more add orange blossom or rose water, stir and cook
for a further 2 minutes. Remove the pan from the heat,
allow to cool slightly, then pour the pudding into a large
glass bowl or individual dishes. Chill and serve, decorated with a pattern of chopped almonds and pistachios.

≈ Some people pour a syrup made of honey boiled with
water and scented with a little orange blossom water
over the cold *muhallabia*

≈ It can also be decorated with crystallized rose petals
or violets, available in many Soho shops.

≈ An unusual and pleasant texture is given by stirring in
120 g (4 oz) ground almonds.

≈ For a stiffer cream increase the amount of ground rice to up to 120 g (4 oz), pour into oiled moulds and turn out just before serving, then decorate with nuts.

≈ When a bowl of *muhallabia* is garnished with little mounds of chopped nuts of different kinds (which can be done in gorgeous patterns) it is so rich that it is called, ironically, 'the dish of the poor' – *keshk el fu'ara*.

KONAFA
Called Kadaif by Greeks and Turks

The dough for this pastry can be bought ready-made in Middle Eastern shops. It is made of flour and water mixed into a liquid batter and poured with a circular motion through a sieve on to a hot metal sheet placed over a small fire. The dough sets in strands which are swept off the sheet very quickly and remain soft. They look like soft white vermicelli.

You can make *konafa* with different fillings. A cream filling, one of walnuts or pistachios and a simple one with a soft cheese are the most common.

500 g (1 lb) konafa pastry
250 g (8 oz) unsalted butter, melted

SYRUP
500 g (1 lb) sugar
300 ml (½ pint) water
2 tablespoons lemon juice
2 tablespoons orange blossom water

FOR A CREAM FILLING
6 tablespoons ground rice
4 tablespoons sugar
1 litre (1¾ pints) milk
150 ml (¼ pint) double cream

FOR A WALNUT OR PISTACHIO FILLING
375 g (12 oz) pistachios or walnuts, coarsely chopped
1 teaspoon cinnamon (optional)

FOR A CHEESE FILLING
1 kg (2 lb) Ricotta

Prepare the syrup by stirring the sugar, water and lemon juice over moderate heat, then simmering until it thickens and coats a spoon. Stir in orange blossom water and cook for 2 minutes longer. Cool and chill in the refrigerater. Prepare either of the following fillings.

Cream filling: mix ground rice and sugar to a smooth paste with ½ cup milk. Boil the rest of the milk and add the ground rice paste stirring vigorously. Simmer, stirring constantly, until very thick. Then allow to cool, add cream and mix well.

Walnut or pitstachio filling: mix the chopped nuts with the cinnamon.

Cheese filling: work the cheese with a fork or with your hands.

Put the *konafa* pastry in a large bowl. Pull out and separate the strands as much as possible with your fingers so that they do not stick together too much. Pour melted butter over them and work it in very thoroughly with your fingers, pulling the shreds and mixing so that each one is entirely coated with butter. Put half the pastry in a large, deep oven dish. Spread the filling over it evenly and cover with the rest of the pastry, evening it out and flattening it with the palm of your hand.

Bake in a preheated slow to moderate oven (160°C/325°F/Mark 3) for 1 hour, then in a hot oven (220°C/425°F/Mark 7) for only 10 to 15 minutes longer, until it is a light golden colour. Remove from the oven and immediately pour half the quantity of the *cold* syrup over the *hot konafa*.

Serve hot or cold with the remaining syrup for people to help themselves if they wish.

SEPHARDI CAKES

Amongst the minority dishes of the Middle East, there are some which are Sephardi Jewish in origin. Besides peculiarities due to their religious dietary laws, such as the use of oil instead of butter or *samna* (clarified butter), the Jews cooked dishes from previous homelands. The main feature of Sephardi cooking as distinct from Middle Eastern cooking is the evidence of Spanish and Portuguese influence.

During the fourteenth and fifteenth centuries, the time of the Inquisition, thousands of Jews left Spain and Portugal after a thousand years of life in the Peninsula. Many headed towards the countries of the Middle East. The local Arab Jews, overwhelmed by their superior intellect, high rank and refined social manners, copied and adopted their liturgy, manners and customs, as well as their dishes. These dishes, similar to those prepared in Spain today – some still bearing Spanish names – are still faithfully prepared by Middle Eastern Jews. Among them are cakes baked specially for the Jewish Passover, made with ground almonds instead of flour.

These cakes, which are half pudding, half cake, can never fail. If they are undercooked they make a fine dessert with cream. They are moist ever to be overcooked or to dry up.

SEPHARDI ORANGE AND ALMOND CAKE

2 large oranges
6 eggs
250 g (8 oz) ground almonds
250 g (8 oz) sugar
1 teaspoon baking powder
Butter and flour, for cake tin

Wash and boil the oranges (unpeeled) in a little water for nearly 2 hours (or ½ hour in a pressure cooker). Let them cool, then cut them open and remove the pips. Turn the oranges into a pulp by rubbing them through a sieve or by putting them in an electric blender or food processor.

Beat the eggs in a large bowl. Add all the other ingredients, mix thoroughly and pour into a buttered and floured cake tin with a removable base if possible. Bake in a preheated moderately hot oven (190°C/375°F/Mark

5) for about 1 hour. If it is still very wet, leave it in the oven for a little longer. Cool in the tin before turning out. This is a very moist cake that may serve as a dessert.

MA'AMOUL
Stuffed Tartlets

Ma'amoul are glorious little stuffed pastries that can have many different shapes and fillings. It is always a thrill to bite into them and to find walnuts, pistachios, almonds or dates. They are an Easter speciality.

An uncle told us of a baking competition organized by a dignitary in Aleppo many years ago. The maker of the best *ma'amoul* would get a prize, to be paid by the dignitary. Hundreds of *ma'amoul* poured into his house, certainly more than the prize was worth, and enough to keep him eating happily for months.

This recipe makes about 40 *ma'amoul*.

500 g (1 lb) plain flour
250 g (8 oz) unsalted butter
2–3 tablespoons orange blossom or rose water
4–5 tablespoons milk or water
Date or Nut Filling (below)
Sifted icing sugar

Sift the flour into a large mixing bowl. Work butter into the flour and mix thoroughly by hand. Add orange blossom or rose water, followed by milk or water – just enough for the dough to hold together – and work until it is soft, malleable and easy to shape.

Take a walnut-sized lump of dough. Roll it into a ball and hollow it out with your thumb. Pinch the sides up to make a pot shape. Fill with either of the two fillings below, then press and pinch the dough back over the filling, making a little ball shape. Place the pastries on a large oven tray. Decorate the tops of the pastries with tweezers or make little dents with a fork. (This will help the icing sugar to cling when they are baked.) Bake in a preheated slow oven (160°C/325°F/Mark 3) for 20 to 25 minutes. Do not let the pastries become brown. They will become hard and their taste will be spoiled. While they are still warm, they will appear soft and uncooked, but on cooling they will become firm.

When cold, roll them in icing sugar. They will keep for a long time in a tightly closed tin.

A simpler version of this is the *ma'amoul* date roll. For this use only the date filling below. Divide the dough into four parts. Roll out and flatten each part into a rectangle 5 cm (2 inches) wide. Spread the filling over each rectangle thinly and roll up lengthwise into thick sausage shapes. Cut diagonally into 3-cm (1¼-inch) sections. Pinch tops or decorate with a fork so that they will hold the sugar better. Bake as above and, when cold, roll in icing sugar.

FILLINGS FOR MA'AMOUL

1. Date Filling

Chop 500 g (1 lb) stoneless dates. Put them in a saucepan with about ½ teacup water. Cook over low heat, stirring, until the dates have softened into a practically homogenous mass. Allow to cool.

2. Nut Filling

*375 g (12 oz) walnuts, almonds or pistachio nuts, finely
    chopped*
1 teaspoon sugar
1 tablespoon rose water or 1 teaspoon ground cinnamon

Mix the chopped nuts with sugar. Add rose water if you are using almonds or pistachios, cinnamon if you are using walnuts. Mix well.

Sherbets and Drinks

SHARBAT

I have long been haunted by the cries and songs of the street vendors in Cairo in my childhood. Most often, it was drinks that they were selling, to quench the thirst of passers-by or, as they sometimes chanted, to give them strength and health. As the vendor went by, people would rush down from their flats to drink several glasses as though the thirst for wine of which Omar Khayyam sang could be quenched by the heavenly sherbets. The vendors carried a selection of sherbets in gigantic glass flasks, two at a time, held together by wide straps and balanced on their shoulders. The flasks glowed with brilliantly seductive colours: soft, pale, sugary pink for rose water, warm, rich, dark tamarind and the purple-black of mulberry juice. As they went through the street, the vendors chanted their traditional, irresistible calls of *'Arasous!'* and *'Tamarhindi!'*, accompanied by the tinkling of little bells and the clanking of the metal cups which they carried with them.

Sherbets or syrups are also served at home at all times of the day, and when guests have already had Turkish coffee and it is time to have something else. A fragrant almond drink and a rose syrup were favourites in my home.

They are very sweet and are meant to be diluted with ice-cold water. A tablespoonful is usually enough for one glass.

YOGHOURT DRINK

An excellent and deliciously refreshing drink, called *abdug* by Persians, *ayran* by the Lebanese, and *laban* by others. It is consumed extensively all over the Middle East and particularly in Turkey and Persia, prepared in homes and cafés, and sold by street vendors.

> *600 ml (1 pint) yoghourt*
> *475–600 ml (¾–1 pint) cold water*
> *Salt*
> *1–3 tablespoons dried crushed mint, or to taste (optional)*

Beat the yoghourt well in a large bowl. Add water and continue to beat vigorously until thoroughly blended together. Use an electric blender if you have one. Season to taste with salt and dried crushed mint if you like.

Serve chilled, preferably with a lump of ice.

KAHWA
Turkish Coffee

Coffee first became popular in the Middle East in the Yemen and Saudi Arabia. The plant was brought to Yemen from Abyssinia, where it grows wild. According to legend, it was particularly favoured by the Yemeni Sufis, who believed that its effects facilitated the performance of their religious ceremonies, hastening mystical raptures. Accordingly, it came to receive a ceremonial character.

Today, the serving and drinking of coffee is still surrounded by tradition and ceremony. Walking past cafés, one cannot help but remark on the almost mystical ecstasy with which coffee-drinking still affects people.

Coffee-drinking is a very important activity in the Middle East. Men spend hours during the long summer nights, and whenever they can during the day, sitting in cafés, sipping coffees one after the other, sometimes accompanied by a *lokum* or pastry, while they sharpen their wits entertaining each other, telling jokes or tales of Goha, setting riddles, and playing charades and *tric-trac* (backgammon).

Business and bargaining are never done without coffee. At home it is served as soon as visitors arrive, always freshly brewed, usually with freshly roasted and pulverized coffee beans. It is always prepared in small quantities as each visitor arrives, in small long-handled copper or brass pots called *kanaka* or *ibrik*, holding from one to five cups.

Coffee cups are very small, usually cylindrical. In some countries they have no handles; in others, china cups fit into small metal holders which match the serving tray made of copper, brass or silver. The tray is usually beautifully ornamented. Traditional patterns and Arabic writing (often blessings and words in praise of God) are chiselled into the metal. Sometimes the carvings are inlaid with a thin silver thread.

People have their favourite blends of coffee beans. Mocha beans from the Yemen are popular, so are Brazilian and Kenya beans.

Rules of etiquette are observed in the serving of coffee. A person of high rank is served first, then a person of advanced age. Until a few years ago, men were always served before women, but today in the more Europeanized towns women take precedence.

Since sugar is boiled at the same time as the coffee, guests are always asked their preference – whether they would like sweet (*helou* or *sukkar ziada*), medium (*mazbout*) or unsweetened (*murra*) – and they are served accordingly. In cafés, it is customary for waiters to take thirty orders for coffee at a time, all varying in sweetness, and supposedly never to make a mistake. There is a well-known joke about the waiter who takes an order for a large gathering of inevitably differing tastes, makes them all exactly the same, medium-sweet, brings them all together on a huge tray and hands them round with a show of concentration, saying: '*Helou, mazbout, helou, murra, murra, helou . . .*'

The occasion may determine the amount of sugar added to the coffee. At happy ones, such as weddings and birthdays, the coffee should always be sweet, while at a funeral it should be bitter, without any sugar at all, regardless of the tastes of the people. At deaths it was customary for some families in Cairo to erect huge tents, which stretched right across the narrow streets. The ground was carpeted and filled with gilt chairs and the tents were decorated with sumptuously coloured appliqués. Relatives, friends and passers-by came to pay their respects. They sat on the gilt chairs, solemnly drinking black, unsweetened coffee to the wailing of the professional mourners.

PER PERSON
1 very heaped teaspoon pulverized coffee
1 heaped teaspoon sugar, or less to taste
1 small coffee cup water

Although it is more common to boil the water and sugar alone first and then add the coffee, it is customary in my family to put the coffee, sugar and water in the *kanaka* or pot (a small saucepan could be used though it is not as successful), and to bring them to the boil together. By a 'very heaped teaspoon' of coffee I mean, in this case so heaped that it is more than 2 teaspoons. A level teaspoon of sugar will make a 'medium' coffee.

Bring to the boil. When the froth begins to rise, remove from the heat, stir, and return to the heat until the froth rises again. Then remove, give the pot a little tap against the side of the stove and repeat once again. Pour immediately into little cups, allowing a little froth (*wesh*) for each cup. (Froth is forced out by making your hand tremble as you serve.) Serve very hot. The grounds will settle at the bottom of the cup. Do not stir them up or drink them.

Try flavouring the coffee with a few drops of orange blossom water, cardamom seeds (called *heil*) or a little cinnamon, adding the flavouring while the coffee is still on the stove top.

≈ It is common practice for people in some circles to turn the coffee cups upside down on their saucers when they have finished drinking. As the coffee grounds dribble down the sides of the cup they form a pattern or image from which at least one member of the company can usually read the fortune of the drinker. A friend has a coffee cup which she brought from Egypt and has kept in a cupboard in England for many years now, carefully wrapped in fine tissue paper and rarely disturbed. She is convinced that it bears the protective image of Rab Moshe (Moses) traced out in coffee grounds at the bottom of the cup.

MOROCCAN MINT TEA

A refreshing infusion of green tea and mint, the preparation of which is considered an art. It is traditionally served in a richly engraved silver pot, and poured from a great height into ornamented glasses. The mint must be of the *mentha viridis* variety. The infusion is sweetened in the teapot.

1½ tablespoons gunpowder green tea
Handful of fresh whole mint leaves
Lump sugar, to taste

Heat the teapot by swirling some boiling water in it and pouring out. Add the tea leaves and pour a little boiling water over them. Swirl round and quickly pour the water out again, taking care not to lose the leaves. Add mint and sugar to taste, and pour in about 1 litre (1½ to 2 pints) of boiling water. Allow to infuse for about 5 to 8 minutes, then skim off any mint that has risen to the surface. Taste a little of the tea in a small glass, and add more sugar if necessary.

Serve in glasses.

GREAT FOOD

NOTES FROM MADRAS
Colonel Wyvern

COLONEL WYVERN, stationed with the army
in Madras during the height of British imperial rule,
opened a cookery school upon his return to England
and was a passionate enthusiast for both
European and Indian cuisine.

In these vivid, common-sense and entertaining
writings, he gives advice on re-creating French classics
in the steaming heat; describes tiffin parties and cooking
while at camp; and laments the declining popularity of
curry in the Raj, providing foolproof recipes for curry
powder, tamarind chutney, korma and 'mulligatunny'
soup. With devotees including Elizabeth David,
Wyvern's unique brand of anglo-Indian cookery is
still reflected in the way we eat today.

*'His recipes are so meticulous and clear, that the
absolute beginner could follow them, yet at the same
time he has much to teach the experienced cook'*
ELIZABETH DAVID

··· GREAT FOOD ···

A TASTE OF THE SUN

Elizabeth David

LEGENDARY COOK AND WRITER Elizabeth David
changed the way Britain ate, introducing a postwar nation
to the sun-drenched delights of the Mediterranean, and
bringing new flavours and aromas such as garlic,
wine and olive oil into its kitchens.

This mouthwatering selection of her writings and
recipes embraces the richness of French and Italian cuisine,
from earthy cassoulets to the simplest spaghetti, as well as
evoking the smell of buttered toast, the colours of foreign
markets and the pleasures of picnics. Rich with anecdote,
David's writing is defined by a passion for good, authentic,
well-balanced food that still inspires chefs today.

*'Above all, Elizabeth David's books
make you want to cook'*
TERENCE CONRAN

GREAT FOOD

EXCITING FOOD FOR SOUTHERN TYPES
Pellegrino Artusi

PELLEGRINO ARTUSI is the original icon of
Italian cookery, whose legendary 1891 book *Science
in the Kitchen and the Art of Eating Well* defined its
national cuisine and is still a bestseller today.

He was also a passionate gastronome, renowned
host and brilliant raconteur, who filled his books with
tasty recipes and rumbustious anecdotes. From an
unfortunate incident regarding minestrone in Livorno
and a proud defence of the humble meat loaf, to
digressions on the unusual history of ice-cream, the
side-effects of cabbage and the Florentines' weak
constitutions, these writings brim with gossip, good
cheer and an inexhaustible zest for life.

'The fountainhead of modern Italian cookery'
GASTRONOMICA

····· GREATFOOD ·····

THE CHEF AT WAR

Alexis Soyer

THE FLAMBOYANT FRENCHMAN Alexis Soyer was
the most renowned chef in Victorian England. This is his
colourful account of his time at the front in the Crimean
War, where he joined British troops in order to improve
the quality of the food they were eating.

Divulging the secrets of preparing stew for 1000
soldiers, sharing sweetmeats with a Turkish Pacha, and
teaching a Highland regiment to cook with his pioneering
gas-fuelled 'field stove' that would be used by armies up
until the Second World War, Soyer gives a vividly
enjoyable lesson in making a little go a long way.

*'The first celebrity chef –
a kind of Anglo/French Jamie Oliver'*
PETER MAY

····· GREAT   FOOD ·····

EATING WITH THE PILGRIMS & OTHER PIECES
Calvin Trillin

ACCLAIMED *NEW YORKER* JOURNALIST, novelist
and poet, Calvin Trillin is also America's funniest and
best-loved writer about food. This selection of some of
his wittiest articles sees him stalking a peripatetic Chinese
chef, campaigning to have the national Thanksgiving dish
changed to spaghetti carbonara and sampling the
legendary Louisiana boudin sausage – to be consumed
preferably 'while leaning against a pickup'.

Eschewing fancy restaurants in favour of street food
and neighbourhood joints, Trillin's writing is a hymn of
praise to the Buffalo chicken wing, the deep-fried
wonton, the New York bagel and the brilliant,
inimitable melting-pot that is US cuisine.

'Marvelously funny and horrifyingly mouth-watering'
ROLLING STONE

GREAT FOOD

A DISSERTATION UPON ROAST PIG & OTHER ESSAYS

Charles Lamb

A RAPTUROUS APPRECIATION of pork crackling, a touching description of hungry London chimney sweeps, a discussion of the strange pleasure of eating pineapple and a meditation on the delights of Christmas feasting are just some of the subjects of these personal, playful writings from early nineteenth-century essayist Charles Lamb.

Exploring the joys of food and also our complicated social relationship with it, these essays are by turns sensuous, mischievous, lyrical and self-mocking. Filled with a sense of hunger, they are some of the most fascinating and nuanced works ever written about eating, drinking and appetite.

'The Georgian essayist, tender and puckish, with a weakness for oddity and alcohol, is one of the great chroniclers of London'
OBSERVER

····· GREAT  FOOD ·····

BUFFALO CAKE AND INDIAN PUDDING

Dr A. W. Chase

TRAVELLING PHYSICIAN, SALESMAN, author and self-made man, Dr Chase dispensed remedies all over America during the late nineteenth century, collecting recipes and domestic tips from the people he met along the way. His self-published books became celebrated US bestsellers and were the household bibles of their day.

Containing recipes for American-style treats, such as Boston cream cakes, Kentucky corn dodgers and pumpkin pie, as well as genial advice on baking bread and testing whether a cake is cooked, this is a treasure trove of culinary wisdom from the homesteads of a still rural, pioneering United States.

····· GREET  FOOD ·····

RECIPES FROM
THE WHITE HART INN
William Verrall

WILLIAM VERRALL, the redoubtable eighteenth-century
landlord of the White Hart Inn in Lewes, Sussex, trained
under a continental chef and was determined to introduce
the 'modern and best French cookery' to his customers.
Gently mocking Englishmen who eat plain mutton chops
or only possess one frying-pan, he gives enthusiastic advice
on must-have kitchen gadgets and describes enticing dishes
such as truffles in French wine and mackerel with fennel.

This selection also includes the recipes that the poet
Thomas Gray scribbled in his own well-thumbed copy
of Verrall's *Complete System of Cookery*, which was one
of the best-loved food books of its time.

'Racily written'
ALAN DAVIDSON

····· GREAT  FOOD ·····

MURDER IN THE KITCHEN
Alice B. Toklas

IN THIS MEMOIR-TURNED-COOKBOOK,
Alice B. Toklas describes her life with partner Gertrude
Stein and their famed Paris salon, which entertained the
great avant-garde and literary figures of their day.

With dry wit and characteristic understatement Toklas
ponders the ethics of killing a carp in her kitchen before
stuffing it with chestnuts; decorating a fish to amuse
Picasso at lunch; and travelling across France during the
First World War in an old delivery truck, gathering
local recipes along the way. She includes a friend's
playful recipe for 'haschiche fudge', which
promises 'brilliant storms of laughter and
ecstatic reveries', much like her book.

*'It will be the fiercest Francophobe who can read
Alice's recipes and not hanker for a taste'*
TIME

GREAT  FOOD

THROUGHOUT the history of civilization, food has been livelihood, status symbol, entertainment – and passion. The twenty fine food writers here, reflecting on different cuisines from across the centuries and around the globe, have influenced each other and continue to influence us today, opening the door to the wonders of every kitchen.